God With Us

Discovering the God of Isaiah

Shirley Byers

*"And this is my prayer:
That your love may abound more and more
In knowledge and depth of insight,
so that you may be able
To discern what is best
And may be pure and blameless
Until the day of Christ,
Filled with the fruit of righteousness,
That comes through Jesus Christ—
To the glory and praise of God."
Philippians 1:9-11*

Introduction

Who is God? What is He like? What does He enjoy and love? What is He passionate about? What does He hate and despise? Does He even have these feelings? What might be His motivation for what He says and does? What is His purpose? What are His plans? And how do we fit into all of this?

> **Who has understood the mind of the Lord, or instructed Him as His counselor?**
> **Isaiah 40:13**

In our humble humanness it is impossible to truly understand the God of the Universe except for what He chooses to reveal to us.

In the Book of Isaiah, God shows us eternal images of Himself to help us understand and grasp who He really is, such as a lamb, a shepherd, a warrior, a savior, and much more. He tells us what He loves and desires, His passions and what angers Him. He clearly longs for a deep, close relationship with mankind and with you.

Whether you are new in your relationship with God or have walked with Him a long time, you can find new treasures of God within the book of Isaiah. Isaiah was a prophet of God who lived 700 years before Jesus Christ, the Savior, during the last days before the Israelites were taken into captivity in Assyria and Babylon. His prophecies were assurances and warnings from God to His people. The focus of this study will not be on the prophet Isaiah, but of the Holy One of Israel, God Almighty, Lord of Hosts who gave him these words.

Do you question whether this God really loves you and really wants to have a relationship with you, that He wants to spend time with you and that He wants you to know Him? Consider the following:

> **I will take you as my own people and I will be
> your God. Then you will know that
> I am the Lord, your God.
> Exodus 6:7**

> **I will give them a heart to know me, that I am the
> Lord. They will be my people and I will be their God,
> for they will return to me with all their heart.
> Jeremiah 24:7**

> **And surely, I am with you always, to the very end of the age.
> Matthew 28:20**

> **Now this is eternal life: that they may know you, the
> Only True God and Jesus Christ, whom You have sent.
> John 17:3.**

> **And Jesus prayed: I have made you known to them and will continue to make you known in order that the love you have for me may be in them and that I myself may be in them (John 17:26).**

> **I pray that you, being rooted and established in love, may
> have the power, together with all the saints, to grasp how
> wide and long and high and deep is the love of Christ,
> and to know this love that surpasses knowledge.
> that you may be filled to the measure of the fullness of God.
> Ephesians 3:17-19**

Yes, the God of the Universe wants to meet with us! He wants to dwell with us and be our God! And God does not want us to just know about Him. He wants us to know Him, really know Him personally and intimately and to love and worship Him. God With Us! To do that, we must spend time with Him and in His Holy Word. Let us delve deeper in our relationship with our God as He reveals Himself in the Book of Isaiah.

My lover spoke and said to me 'Arise my darling,
my beautiful one and come with me.'
Song of Songs 2:10

Come, let us meet with God. He is waiting for us.

Let My teaching fall like rain and My words descend like dew,
like showers on new grass, like abundant
rain on tender plants.
Deuteronomy 32:2

God's Plan and our Attitude

Lesson 1: Isaiah Chapters 1-2

This week's memory verse:

> **But the plans of the Lord stand firm forever,**
> **the purposes of His heart through all generations.**
> **Psalm 33:11**

Before you begin: Please start by praying to God. Give Him praise. Ask Him to reveal Himself and to speak to you today through this lesson.

What is God's plan for us? What is His will for my life? Good authors or orators will give you a preview of what they are going to tell you, then tell you the information, and then summarize what they told you. In this first chapter, God gives us a preview of the book of Isaiah and His plan for all mankind. In the second chapter He instructs us on the right attitude to have whenever we approach the Throne of God, which is with humility and awe.

Please read Isaiah Chapter 1.

1) What do **verses 2-4** tell us about the relationship between God and man?

God created man and we rebelled against Him.

2) List some of the things that displeases God, that He even hates, found in **verses 10-16** and **21-23**.

3) What does God ask us to do in **verses 16-17**?

4) No one unclean, impure and with sin can enter into the presence of God. God wants us to be with Him, so He had a plan. His plan is revealed in **verse 18**. Look up the following verses. What has God done for us?

Jeremiah 33:8—

Hebrews 9:22 and 28—

Hebrews 10:10—

I John 1:7—

> **I will thoroughly purge away your dross
> and remove all your iniquities.
> Isaiah 1:25**

5) Read **verses 24-27**. What does the City of Righteousness represent? Please also see **Zechariah 8:3** and **Revelation 21:2** and **10**.

6) What has God planned for those who do not worship Him? See **verses 28-31** and **Revelation 20:11-15** and **Revelation 21:8**.

In this first chapter of Isaiah, God reveals His plan for all mankind. God created man. Man rebelled against God. God sent His Son as a sacrifice to cleanse and atone for man's sin. For those who obey Him, God promises eternal life with Him in His Holy City. For those who rebel against Him, God promises an unquenchable fire.

How much more then will the blood of Christ, who through the Eternal Spirit, offered Himself unblemished to God, cleanse our consciences from acts that lead to death, so that we may serve the Living God.
Hebrews 9:14

God has shown us His plan for mankind. He now teaches us to have the right attitude as we enter into His presence and study His Word.

Please read Isaiah Chapter 2.

7) How does God describe Himself in **verses 10, 19**, and **21**? Using a dictionary, define "Majesty." What do **Psalm 93:1** and **Hebrews 1:3** tell us about this aspect of God?

8) What words are used to describe the men God will destroy in verses **11, 12**, and **17**? What does this tell you about God? What do we learn about God in **Proverbs 6:16-19** and **Jeremiah 9:23-24**?

9) Read **2 Chronicles 26:16-21**. How was King Uzziah described? What did he try to do? What happened to him?

10) We tend to separate between "us" and "them." In reality, if we are honest with ourselves, we are all a little like "them," arrogant and prideful at times. With this in mind, describe a time when you were arrogant and prideful. What happened?

11) According to verses **11-12**, what will happen to the men who are arrogant and prideful?

12) Look up the following verses: **Psalm 145:14, Isaiah 66:2, Matthew 5:5**, and **James 4:10**. Who does God esteem?

13) What do **verses 11** and **17** tell us about God, compared to those who are arrogant?

14) What have we learned about God in this chapter? About ourselves? What should be our response? See **Ephesians 4:1-2** and **I Peter 5:6**.

> **My heart is not proud, O Lord, my eyes are not haughty; I do not concern myself with great matter or things too wonderful for me. But I have still and quieted my soul; like a weaned child with its mother, like a weaned child is my soul within me. O Israel, put your hope in the Lord both now and forevermore.**
> **Psalm 131**

15) Knowing that God has a plan and a purpose for all His creation from the beginning to the end, what do you think is God's purpose and plan for you? He has designed His creation in tiny, minute detail. Can you trust Him with the details of your life, even the minor ones?

Before you go: Consider how the Lord specifically revealed Himself to you today. What words or phrases caught your attention? How do you respond to this? Lift a prayer of praise to the Lord.

Further Thoughts:

In the last days, the mountain of the Lord's temple will be established as chief among the mountains; it will be raised above the hills, and all nations will stream to it.
Isaiah 2:2

The Holy Mountain of the Lord, Mount Zion, the City of Righteousness, the Holy City, the City of Zion, Jerusalem, will be described many times throughout the Book of Isaiah.
What does the Mountain of God, the City of Zion in the last days represent? What do the following verses say about this place?

Isaiah 11:9-10—

Isaiah 25:6-8—

Isaiah 35:10—

Isaiah 56:6-7—

Isaiah 65:25—

Psalm 48—

Micah 4:1-7—

**The moon will be abashed, the sun ashamed;
for the Lord Almighty will reign on
Mount Zion and in Jerusalem, and before its elders, gloriously.
Isaiah 24:23**

Beautiful Images of the Lord

Lesson 2: Isaiah Chapters 3-5

This week's memory verse:

> **Great is the Lord and most worthy of praise.**
> **His greatness no one can fathom.**
> **Psalm 145:3.**

Before you begin: Please start by praying to God. Give Him praise. Ask Him to reveal Himself and to speak to you today through this lesson.

In these early chapters of Isaiah, God shows us who He is, His roles and His character by using several images. Let us discover some of the beauty and wonder of our God.

Please read Isaiah Chapters 3 and 4.

1) What is the name given to God in the first verse? What does this tell us about God? In **Chapter 3** God warns His people of the devastation that is about to happen because of their sins. He reveals His mighty power. He is Omnipotent! He is the Lord of Hosts, the Lord Almighty! Nothing can thwart what He has planned. He is capable of doing what He says He will do. Read **Job 11:7-9**. Why is this characteristic of God important?

2) . . . *their words and deeds are against the Lord, defying His glorious presence* (**Isaiah 3:8**). Read **Psalm 99:1** and **Nahum 1:5**. How does the earth respond to the Presence of God?

God's presence is so awesome, the earth trembles! Yet, Jerusalem and Judah did not. God's people lost their fear and awe of the Mighty, Holy God of Israel.

> **The fear of the Lord is the beginning of knowledge,**
> **but fools despise wisdom and discipline.**
> **Proverbs 1:7**

3) Read the following verses: **Jude 24-25** and **Hebrews 4:16**. What has Jesus done for us? How should we respond to this? See **Psalm 16:11 and Psalm 96:9**.

> **Jesus answered, 'I am the way, the truth and the life.**
> **No one comes to the Father except through me.'**
> **John 14:6**

4) What role does God take in **Isaiah 3:13-14**? What are your thoughts and feelings about God being a Judge? Does it bring comfort or fear? Consider the following verses: **Psalm 7:8-9, Psalm 94:2,** and **2 Corinthians 5:10**.

5) **Isaiah 3:16 - 4:1** speaks specifically to women. Is it wrong to wear jewelry or perfume or to fix your hair? What separates these women from those who please God? See **I Timothy 2:9-10** and **I Peter 3:3-4**.

> **The Lord does not look at the things man looks at. Man looks at the outward appearance, but the Lord looks at the heart.**
> **I Samuel 16:7**

6) The Branch of the Lord, Root or Shoot of David is a Messianic title in the Old Testament. What do these verses tell you about The Branch: **Isaiah 11:1, Isaiah 53:2, Jeremiah 23:5,** and **Jeremiah 33:15**. How does **Isaiah 4:2** describe the Branch of the Lord?

7) The Lord himself will wash away, cleanse the impurities of man through a **Spirit of Judgment and a Spirit of Fire (Isaiah 4:4)**. What do these verses tell us about God? **Isaiah 48:10**, and **Zechariah 13:9**. According to **Hebrews 12:5-11**, how does God refine us?

8) When God was with the Israelites in the desert, He revealed Himself as a Pillar of Cloud and a Pillar of Fire (see **Exodus 13:21**). **It will be a shelter and shade from the heat of the day, and a refuge and hiding place from the storm and rain (Isaiah 4:6)**. Describe a time when God has been a shelter or refuge for you.

> **The Lord watches over you–the Lord is your shade at your right hand; the sun will not harm you by day, nor the moon by night. The Lord will keep you from all harm–He will watch over your life; the Lord will watch over your coming and going both now and forevermore.**
> **Psalm 121:5-8**

Oh, the Glorious Presence of Our Lord! He has revealed Himself in so many ways in this Lesson. He is the Almighty, the Lord of Hosts, our Provider, our Strength, The Holy One, our Savior, our Judge, our Purifier, our Disciplining Father, our Guide, our Shelter, and our Light!

Let us look at another beautiful image of our God –The Gardener.

> **I will sing of the one I love a song about His vineyard. My loved one had a vineyard...**
> **Isaiah 5:1**

Please read Isaiah Chapter 5.

9) Have you ever planted a garden? What specific tasks do gardeners do to care for their garden?

10) God has a vineyard. He is the Gardener. Who does the vineyard, the "garden of His delight" represent according to **verse 7**? What words or phrases describe God's love and tenderness for His vineyard?

> **Then He looked for a crop of good grapes, but it yielded only bad fruit.**
> **Isaiah 5:2**

11) God poured out His love into His vineyard, yet it only produced "bad fruit." What was His response? What was God's response in **Jeremiah 12:7** and **10-13**?

> **For a brief moment, I abandoned you, but with
> deep compassion I will bring you back.
> Isaiah 54:7**

12) What hope do we find in **Jeremiah 12:14-16** and **Hosea 14:4-7?**

13) God's people cry out to Him in **Psalm 80:8-19**. What are they asking God to do?

> **Watch over this vine, the root Your right hand has
> planted, the son You have raised up for Yourself. . . Let
> your hand rest on the man at Your right hand,
> the son of man You have raised up for Yourself.
> Psalm 80:15 and 17**

14) According to **Acts 2: 32-36**, who is the "son of man" found in **Psalm 80**?

15) Read **John 15:1-17**. Who is the gardener? How does Jesus describe Himself? What is our relationship to Jesus? How is God's love for us shown in these verses?

> **As the Father has loved me, I have loved you.
> John 15:9**

> **Greater love has no one that this, that he
> lay down his live for his friends.
> You are my friends.**

John 15:13-14

**But I chose you and appointed you to go and
bear fruit--fruit that will last.**
John 15:16

16) Read **Song of Songs 4:12-5:1** and **6:2-3**. What does God desire to do in His garden?

God is the Gardener, and we are His garden of delight! He desires to linger in His garden and savor the bountiful fruit! He finds pleasure in spending time with us!

**I will sing for the one I love a song about His
vineyard: My loved one had a vineyard...**
Isaiah 5:1

17) Which of these beautiful images of God are meaningful to you today? Write a prayer of praise to God.

Before you go: Consider how the Lord specifically revealed Himself to you today. What words or phrases caught your attention? How do you respond to this? Lift a prayer of praise to the Lord.

Further Thoughts:

1) **Those who are left in Zion, who remain in Jerusalem, will be called holy...** (Isaiah 4:3). Define "holy" using a dictionary. Read **I Peter 1:15-16**. How can we meet this expectation? Continue reading **I Peter 1:18-19**.

2) We are described as God's delightful garden. How do the following verses add to this vision?

Psalm 1:3—

Psalm 52:8—

Isaiah 58:11—

Isaiah 61:3b—

Jeremiah 17:7-8—

> **I am the vine; you are the branches. If anyone
> remains in me and I in him,
> he will bear much fruit...
> John 15:5**

3) Review the "woes" in **Isaiah Chapter 5**, things that distress and anger God. It seems like Isaiah is describing our world today. Does God speak to you in any way in these verses? If so, write your thoughts.

The Holy God, Emmanuel, Light of the World

Lesson 3: Isaiah Chapters 6-9

This week's memory verse:

> **Holy, holy, holy is the Lord Almighty; the whole earth is full of His glory.**
> **Isaiah 6:3**

Before you begin: Please start by praying to God. Give Him praise. Ask Him to reveal Himself and to speak to you today through this lesson.

In these significant chapters, Isaiah has the honor and privilege to enter the Throne Room of God, to be in His presence, and to see God Himself! Let us discover the Holy God as revealed through the eyes of Isaiah and others who have had this honor.

Isaiah willingly accepts the task of being God's messenger. And what amazing messages God has for us! Messages that were not only for God's people at that time, but for us today and future generations and for all of eternity!

Please read Isaiah Chapter 6.

1) What are some of the things Isaiah saw and experienced while in the presence of the Lord Almighty?

2) There are others who also have been in God's presence. Please

look up the following scriptures and describe what they saw and experienced. What words are used to describe God? What does His Throne Room look like? Who is present with Him?

Ezekiel—**Ezekiel 1:25-28**:

Daniel—**Daniel 7:9, 13-14**:

John—**Revelation 1:9-18, 4:1-11**:

3) What words are used to describe God in **verse 3**? How is this significant? How is Jesus described in the following verses? **Luke 1:35** and **Luke 4:34**?

4) What was Isaiah's response when he entered the Presence of God? (**vs. 5**). How did Ezekiel, Daniel, and John respond? Why do you think they responded in this way? How do you think you would respond?

Ezekiel—**Ezekiel 3:15**:

Daniel—**Daniel 7:28**:

John—**Revelation 1:17**:

Whenever we step into the Presence of God, we are awestruck by His Holiness and humbled by our impurities. **Woe to me! I am ruined! For I am a man of unclean lips! (Isaiah 6:5)**. However, we have a Merciful God who welcomes us. He has made a way for us.

> **If You, O Lord kept a record of sins, O Lord, who could stand? But with You there is forgiveness, therefore You are feared.**
> **Psalm 130:3-4**

5) In **verse 8**, God asks **And who will go for us?** Who might be included in **"us?"** What do we learn about God in the following verses? **Genesis 1:26, I Kings 22:19-20, Psalm 89:5-7,** and **Revelation 4:4?**

God is a mystery! After Isaiah said, **"Here am I. Send me!"** God gave him a strange message to share with His people. We are not capable of fully understanding God. If we were, then there would be no need for faith. Faith requires trust in the unknown.

> **Now faith is being sure of what we hope for**
> **and certain of what we do not see.**
> **Hebrews 11:1**

6) Within this mystery, God gives us hope. What hope do we find in **verse 13**? **Isaiah 11:1** gives us a clearer picture.

God will bring His people back. The stump of Israel will bud and flourish and the Holy Seed, the Messiah will rise up.

> **In Him (Jesus) and through faith in Him**
> **we may approach God with**
> **freedom and confidence.**
> **Ephesians 3:12**

> **But I, by Your great mercy, will come into**
> **Your house; in reverence,**
> **will I bow down toward Your holy temple.**
> **Psalm 5:7**

> **I love the house where You live, O Lord, the**
> **place where Your glory dwells.**
> **Psalm 26:8**

Please read Isaiah Chapter 7 and 2 Kings 16:1 - 17:6.

The virgin will be with child and will give birth to a son and will call him Emmanuel.
Isaiah 7:14

God gives a sign, a prophecy to King Ahaz, a word of assurance to him, that also becomes a well-known assurance for us, because Jesus Christ was born of a virgin. Many times in Isaiah, God's prophecies have more than one meaning. Let us look at this one more closely.

7) Describe what happens in **verse 1** and **2 Kings 16:5**.

The two kings plotted against King Ahaz of Judah, and they failed. **It will not take place; it will not happen** (Isaiah 7:7).

8) What does God tell King Ahaz will happen to these two kings in **verses 16-17**?

9) What happens to them in **2 Kings 17:5-6**?

Here we see a prophecy of God given and the prophecy fulfilled. God assured King Ahaz that even though an invasion is coming, in the time for a young woman to conceive and give birth to a child, God will be with him, and he and the land of Judah will be secure. The Assyrians invaded the land of Israel and captured the people and took them to Assyria. It will be about 150 years later when the Babylonians invade and capture Judah.

10) Read **Matthew 1:18-25**. What was the name given to Jesus in **verse 23**? What does this name mean?

God sends Jesus, the Messiah and gives Him the name Emmanuel—God With Us! The Awesome God who created the universe wants to be with us!

> **What is man that You are mindful of him?**
> **Psalm 8:4**

> **Lord, You have been our dwelling place**
> **throughout all generations.**
> **Psalm 90:1**

11) What does Jesus promise us in **Matthew 28:20**? What is His desire for us in **John 14:3, 20** and **23**? And what does Jesus ask God for in **John 17:20-26**?

12) Read **Acts 17:24-28**. Why did God create us? How does God describe the intimacy we can have with Him in **verse 28**? What are your thoughts about the Emmanuel God wanting to be with you?

> **Now the dwelling of God is with men, and He will**
> **live with them. They will be His people and God**
> **Himself will be with them and be their God.**
> **Revelation 21:3**

Please read Isaiah Chapter 8.

> **He will call upon me and I will answer him,**
> **I will be with him in trouble,**
> **I will deliver him and honor him.**
> **Psalm 91:15**

13) In **verses 5-10** God again tells His people that nations will attack and overcome them because they rejected Him. He uses the image of mighty floodwaters. But God also gives a glimpse of hope. What is God's name in **verse 8**? And what does He remind them in **verse 10**?

14) Describe a time in your life when you felt overwhelmed. Can you also see that God was with you during this time? Why or why not? What assurances do we find in **Psalm 55:22** and **I Peter 5:7**?

15) Read **verses 11-18**. Let us look at the following descriptions of God in these verses.

> **God is holy.** He is to be feared. He is the one to dread. What does it mean to fear God? What does **Hebrews 12:28** tell us to do?

> **God is a sanctuary.** What assurance and comfort do we find in **Psalm 91**?

> **God is a rock, a trap and a snare.** These are unusual ways to describe God. Consider these verses to give us some insight: **Isaiah 28:16, Romans 9:30-33, I Corinthians 1:22-25** and **I Peter 2:4-8**.

> Great peace have they who love Your law, and
> nothing can make them stumble.
> **Psalm 119:165**

16) What is God's opinion of mediums, witches, and sorcery according to **Leviticus 19:31** and **Deuteronomy 18:10-12**?

What does God want us to do in **verse 19** and **James 1:5**?

> **Oh, the depth of the riches of the wisdom and knowledge of God! How unsearchable His judgments, and His paths beyond tracing out!**
> **Romans 11:33**

> **My help comes from the Lord, the Maker of Heaven and earth. He will not let your foot slip.**
> **Psalm 121:2-3**

Please read Isaiah Chapter 9.

> **The people walking in darkness have seen a great light; on those living in the land of the shadow of death a light has dawned.**
> **Isaiah 9:2**

"Nevertheless." This is a continuation from **Chapter 8.** "If they do not speak according to this word, they have no light of dawn... They will... see only distress and darkness and fearful gloom and they will be thrust into utter darkness." **Isaiah 8:20-22**. The people have turned away from God and now they are in despair. They have no hope. Thankfully, our God is a God of mercy and compassion. He gives us hope.

17) What hope do we find in **Luke 2:30-32** and **John 1:1-9**?

> **I am the Light of the World. Whoever follows Me will never walk in darkness, but will have the light of life.**
> **John 8:12**

> **I have come into the world as a light, so that no one who believes in Me should stay in darkness.**

John 12:46

> You, O Lord, keep my lamp burning; my God
> turns my darkness into light.
> Psalm 18:28

> For you have delivered me from death
> and my feet from stumbling,
> that I may walk before God in the light of life.
> Psalm 56:13

18) What action does God take in **verse 4**? What are our burdens? What is our burden according to **Psalm 38:4**? What does Jesus ask us to do in **Matthew 11:28-30**?

In **verse 4**, God "**shattered the yoke that burdens them.**" He does not just take our burdens away, He obliterates them!

19) What is the precious promise God gives us in **verses 6-7**?

> Today in the town of David a Savior has been
> born to you; His is Christ the Lord.
> Luke 2:11

> This is how God showed His love among us: He sent His one and only Son into the world that we might live through Him. This is love: not that we loved God, but that He loved us and sent His Son as an atoning sacrifice for our sins.
> I John 4:9-10

20) **The zeal of the Lord Almighty will accomplish this** (**Isaiah 9:7**). Define the word "**zeal**." What will God zealously accomplish? What does this characteristic of God mean to you?

Before you go: Consider how the Lord specifically revealed Himself to you today. What words or phrases caught your attention? How do you respond to this? Lift a prayer of praise to the Lord.

Further Thoughts:

Define the following words using a dictionary. What insights do you find as you pair the words together? How is the Trinity—Father, Son, and Holy Spirit shown in these verses?

Wonderful—

Counselor—

Mighty—

God—

Everlasting—

Father—

Prince—

Peace—

A Trustworthy God, A Banner, and A Fountain of Living Water

Lesson 4: Isaiah Chapters 10-12

This week's memory verse:

> **If anyone acknowledges that Jesus is the Son of God, God lives in him and he in God. And so, we know and rely on the love God has for us.**
> **I John 4:15-16**

Before you begin: Please start by praying to God. Give Him praise. Ask Him to reveal Himself and to speak to you today through this lesson.

The God who created the heavens and the earth is powerful and capable. He also has immeasurable love for each of us. How can we not trust Him in every circumstance? And yet we waver sometimes. Fear takes a hold of us, and we doubt God's capability or willingness.

Please read Isaiah Chapter 10.

1) Who is God concerned about in **verses 1-2**?

> **A father to the fatherless, a defender of widows, is God in His holy dwelling.**
> **Psalm 68:5**

2) In **verse 5** God focuses His anger on Assyria who has been

oppressing God's people. What do the Assyrians say about themselves in **verses 13-14**? What does God say about this in **verse 15**? Who is really in control?

3) In **verse 20** we see that God's people returned to the Lord and began to truly rely on The Holy One of Israel. What does God promise He will do for them in **verses 25-27**?

> **Trust in the Lord with all your heart and lean not on your own understanding; in all your ways acknowledge Him and He will make your paths straight.**
> **Proverbs 3:5-6**

4) God's desire is for us to trust Him completely. Do you rely on God fully? What areas of your life are you holding on to? What is God's promise for us in **Proverbs 20:22**?

> **May the God of hope fill you with all joy and peace as you trust in Him, so that you may overflow with hope by the power of the Holy Spirit.**
> **Romans 15:13**

Please read Isaiah Chapter 11.

This chapter is a prophecy of Jesus Christ the Messiah and our future heavenly home. Jesse was the father of King David. The Messiah was called the Son of David. **So the holy seed will be the stump in the land (Isaiah 6:13) and He will reign on David's throne.**

5) What do we learn about Jesus in **verses 1-2**? What do the following verses tell us about Jesus? **Matthew 7:28-29, Luke 2:47** and **52**, and **Colossians 2:2-3**.

> **Worthy is the Lamb who was slain, to receive
> power and wealth and wisdom
> and strength and honor and glory and praise!
> Revelation 5:12**

6) When Jesus was on earth, He was mostly gentle and peaceful. The only anger He showed was when He cleared the Temple (**Mark 11:15-17**). In **verses 4-5** Jesus is a warrior. How is Jesus described in **Psalm 2** and **Revelation 19:11-21**? Do these images of Jesus bring you comfort or fear?

Jesus Christ, the Messiah is powerful and able to defeat all the evils of Satan in this final battle! Hallelujah!

7) Define the word "banner" using a dictionary. **In that day the Root of Jesse will stand as a banner for the peoples (verse 10).** How is Jesus like a banner?

> **His banner over me is love.
> Song of Songs 2:4**

8) In **verses 6-16** we have a glimpse of our Heavenly home, a place of peace. Also read **Ezekiel 37:24-28** and **Micah 5:4**. What aspects of our Heavenly home do you look forward to?

> **Lord, You have assigned me my portion and my cup; You have made my lot secure. The boundary lines have fallen for me in pleasant places; surely, I have a delightful**

> inheritance . . . You have made known to me the path of life; You will fill me with joy in Your presence, with eternal pleasures at Your right hand.
> Psalm 16:5-6, 11

Please read Isaiah Chapter 12.

"**In that day . . .**" a continuation from the last two chapters. This is a praise song to God! It is possible that it is one we will sing to Him when we are in heaven with Him!

> But You, O Lord are a compassionate and gracious God, slow to anger, abounding in love and faithfulness.
> Psalm 86:15

9) Describe a time when God was—

Your salvation—

Your strength—

Your song—

> O my Strength, I will sing praise to You; You O God are my fortress, my loving God.
> Psalm 59:17

10) **With joy you will draw water from the wells of salvation (Isaiah 12:3).** How does God describe Himself in **Jeremiah 2:13**? What does Jesus say in **John 4:10** and **14**?

> As the deer pants for streams of water, so my soul pants for You, O God. My soul thirsts for God, for the living God. When can I go and meet with God?

Psalm 42:1-2

11) How does God describe the place where He lives in the following verses? **Psalm 36:8-9, Psalm 46:4, Revelation 7:17** and **Revelation 22:1-2**.

12) What does this Fountain of Life/Well of Salvation symbolize? Look up the following verses for further insight: **Ezekiel 36:25, Ephesians 5:26, Titus 3:5-6** and **I Peter 3:21**.

> **O God, you are my God, earnestly I seek You, my soul thirsts for You, my body longs for You in a dry and weary land where there is no water.**
> **Psalm 63:1**

> **He leads me beside the quiet waters.**
> **Psalm 23:2**

Before you go: Consider how the Lord specifically revealed Himself to you today. What words or phrases caught your attention? How do you respond to this? Lift a prayer of praise to the Lord.

Further Thoughts:

1) In Chapter 10, the Assyrians were arrogant and believed in their own power. How did Satan tempt Eve in **Genesis 3:4-5**? Who did she want to be like? Why did the people want to build

a tower in **Genesis 11:4**? Why did Simon the Sorcerer want the same gifts as the apostles in **Acts 8:18-23**?

2) Has there ever been a time when you maybe tried to solve a problem on your own first without consulting God? Or you believed you were entitled to something? Maybe there was a time when you were a little bit selfish or prideful? Are we not a little like Eve sometimes? Or the people who tried to build the tower to heaven? Or dare I say, even a little like Satan himself? What should be our right attitude? What do we learn from **James 3:13-4:10**?

The Awesome, Powerful and Merciful God

Lesson 5: Isaiah Chapters 13-16

This week's memory verse:

**In love a throne will be established; in faithfulness a man will sit on it—one from the house of David—one who in judging seeks justice and speeds the cause of righteousness.
Isaiah 16:5**

Before you begin: Please start by praying to God. Give Him praise. Ask Him to reveal Himself and to speak to you today through this lesson.

Please read Isaiah Chapter 13.

Oh the furious, powerful wrath of God! Who is this frightening God? Why is He so angry? How can such a loving God show such fury? As we look closer, we will be able to understand that God's wrath is an expression of love for us.

> **For God did not appoint us to suffer wrath
> but to receive salvation through
> our Lord Jesus Christ.
> I Thessalonians 5:9**

1) Read **2 Chronicles 36:15-20, Psalm 79:1-4,** and **Revelation 18:1-8** and **24**. Why is God so angry with Babylon?

2) How does God display His power in **verses 9-10** and **13**? How does He display His power in **Psalm 97:1-6, Psalm 102:25-27** and **Nahum 1:2-6**?

> **May God arise, may His enemies be scattered; may His foes flee before Him. As smoke is blown away by the wind, may You blow them away; as wax melts before the fire, may the wicked perish before God.**
> **Psalm 68:1-2**

3) Who does God's wrath fall upon in **verse 11**? Who does **Romans 1:18-2:10** say will experience God's wrath?

> **See, the Sovereign Lord comes with power and His arm rules for Him. See His reward is with Him, and His recompense accompanies Him.**
> **Isaiah 40:10**

> **Then the end will come, when He (Christ) hands over the kingdom to God the Father after He has destroyed all dominion, authority and power. For He must reign until He has put all His enemies under His feet.**
> **I Corinthians 15:24-25**

4) Yes, our Almighty God is awesome and powerful and full of wrath! But can you also see His overwhelming love? How does God show His love in **2 Peter 3:7-13**?

> **The Lord reigns forever; He has established His throne for judgment. He will judge the world in**

> righteousness... Those who know Your Name will trust in You, for You Lord, have never forsaken those who seek You. Sing praises to the Lord, enthroned in Zion; proclaim among the nations what He has done.
> **Psalm 9:7-11**

Please read Isaiah Chapter 14.

> **The Lord will have compassion on Jacob; once again He will choose Israel and will settle them in their own land. Aliens will join them and unite with the house of Jacob.**
> **Isaiah 14:1**

5) God promises to bring His people back to His Holy Mountain. Who do you think are these aliens or strangers who will unite with them? Read again **Isaiah 11:10** and **Isaiah 49:6**.

> **Go and make disciples of all nations...**
> **Matthew 28:19**

> **This is what is written: The Christ will suffer and rise from the dead on the third day and repentance and forgiveness of sins will be preached in His name to all nations beginning at Jerusalem.**
> **Luke 24:46-47**

6) Read **verses 12-15**. Who has fallen from heaven? What did Jesus say in **Luke 10:18**? See also **Ezekiel 28:11-19** and **Revelation 12:7-9**. What did he want to do? What was his attitude? What will happen to him? What is his ultimate end in **Revelation 20:10**?

> **To fear the Lord is to hate evil. I hate pride and arrogance,**

> **evil behavior and perverse speech.**
> **Proverbs 8:13**

7) What does God tell us about Himself in **verses 24** and **27**?

God is God. He is in control. He has the power and the wisdom. He has the compassion and mercy. He is trustworthy.

> **You are worthy, our Lord and God, to receive glory and honor and power, for You created all things, and by Your will they were created and have their being.**
> **Revelation 4:11**

> **For the Lord takes delight in His people; He crowns the humble with salvation.**
> **Psalm 149:4**

Please read Isaiah Chapter 15 and 16.

This is a lament, an expression of grief and sadness over death and destruction of Moab, a country bordering Israel and Judah. Even though God commanded the destruction because of their sin, He still grieves over the loss of the people He created. And in the midst of this sadness, God again gives us hope.

8) Look a little closer at **verses 15:5**, and **16:9, 11**. What emotions does God express? Yes, it is God who is speaking, not Isaiah. **Isaiah 15:9** tells us "**But I will still bring more upon Dimon.**" Isaiah is not bringing more destruction; God is, so it is God speaking these words. Have you ever wept deeply for someone?

> **My heart cries out... So, I weep... I drench you with tears! My heart laments for Moab like a**

> **harp, my inmost being for Kir Hareseth.**
> **Isaiah 15:5 and 16:9, 11**

Oh, the amazing love of God!

9) What is the promise God gives us in **16:5**? What word is used to describe how the throne will be established? What word is used to describe how a man will sit on the throne?

10) What does God promise in **2 Samuel 7:12-16**? How does Jesus Christ, the Messiah fulfill this prophecy? What does Jesus tell His disciples in **Matthew 19:28**?

> **He will reign on David's throne and over his kingdom, establishing and upholding it with justice and righteousness from that time on and forever.**
> **Isaiah 9:7**

11) Read **Revelation 5:5-6**, **Revelation 7:17**, and **Revelation 22:1**. Who is sitting on the throne?

> **The Son is the radiance of God's glory and the exact representation of His being, sustaining all things by His powerful word. After He had provided purification for sins, He sat down at the right hand of the Majesty in heaven.**
> **Hebrews 1:3**

> **But about the Son He says, 'Your throne, O God, will last forever and ever.'**
> **Hebrews 1:8**

Before you go: Consider how the Lord specifically revealed Himself to you today. What words or phrases caught your attention? How do you respond to this? Lift a prayer of praise to the Lord.

Further Thoughts: Describe a time when God showed His power in your life? How has He shown His mercy?

The Rock, the Quiet Observer, the Capturer

Lesson 6: Isaiah Chapters 17-20

This week's memory verse:

> **We wait in hope for the Lord; He is our help and our shield. In Him our hearts rejoice, for we trust in His holy name. May Your unfailing love rest upon us, O Lord, even as we put our hope in You.**
> **Psalm 33:20-22**

Before you begin: Please start by praying to God. Give Him praise. Ask Him to reveal Himself and to speak to you today through this lesson.

Please read Isaiah Chapter 17.

In this chapter, we see that there are two groups of people. One acknowledges the Lord their Maker for who He is and seeks Him instead of the false gods around them. The other has forgotten God, his Savior, and suffers the consequences of losing His love and protection.

> **In that day men will look to their Maker and turn their eyes to the Holy One of Israel.**
> **Isaiah 17:7**

1) What do the following verses tell us about our Creator, Maker? What does He want us to do?

Job 33:4—

Psalm 95:6—

Psalm 139:13-14—

Psalm 149:2—

Ecclesiastes 12:1—

> **Do you not know? Have you not heard? The Lord is the everlasting God, the Creator or the ends of the earth. Isaiah 40:28**

--o--

> **You have forgotten God your Savior, you have not remembered the Rock, your fortress. Isaiah. 17:10**

> **You deserted the Rock, who fathered you; you forgot the God who gave you birth. Deuteronomy 32:18**

2)   What does it mean for God to be a Rock, a Fortress, a Stronghold? How does the psalmist describe God in these verses? **Psalm 18:2, Psalm 62:2,** and **Psalm 71:3**? How has He been this for you? How can we keep from "forgetting our Rock?"

3) Read **Matthew 7:24-27**. What do we learn from Jesus' parable in light of God being our Rock?

> **Come, let us sing for joy to the Lord; let us shout aloud to the Rock of our salvation. Let us come before Him with thanksgiving and extol Him with music and song. For**

the Lord is the great God, the great King above all gods. In His hand are the depths of the earth, and the mountain peaks belong to Him. The sea is His, for he made it, and His hands formed the dry land. Come, let us bow down in worship, let us kneel before the Lord our Maker.
Psalm 95:1-6

Please read Isaiah Chapter 18.

Sometimes it seems God is quiet and aloof. He does not seem to be answering our prayers and He does not seem to be concerned about all the evil and sickness in our world. But God is doing something very significant. There is value in rest and quiet. Let us learn from His example.

4) What significant event is described in **verse 3**? What does **Matthew 24:30-31** and **I Thessalonians 4:16-17** tell us about this event?

I will remain quiet and will look on from My dwelling place.
Isaiah 18:4

5) There are times when it seems God is quiet and inactive. What do the following verses tell us that He is doing?

2 Chronicles 16:9—

Psalm 33:13-14, 18—

Psalm 34:15—

Proverbs 15:3—

> **The fruit of the Spirit is. . . patience. . .gentleness
> and self-control.
> Galatians 5:22-23**

6) The Lord is patiently waiting. He will move in His perfect wisdom and timing. What do these verses tell us about God's patience? **Romans 2:4, I Timothy 1:15-16,** and **2 Peter 3:8-9?**

> **Love is patient. . .
> I Corinthians 13:4**

7) If God is waiting patiently, what should we also do? Consider **Psalm 37:7** and **Psalm 40:1.**

> **Wait for the Lord; be strong and take
> heart and wait for the Lord.
> Psalm 27:14**

> **In repentance and rest is your salvation, in
> quietness and trust is your strength.
> Isaiah 30:15**

8) **Like shimmering heat in the sunshine, like a cloud of dew in the heat of harvest (Isaiah 18:4).** We have all seen a shimmer of heat and the moist morning dew. What are your thoughts about these images of God?

> **And these are but the outer fringe of His works,
> how faint the whisper we hear of Him!**
> **Job 26:14**

9) According to **verse 7**, where is the place of the Name of the Lord? What is the significance of His Name in this place?

Please read Isaiah Chapter 19.

    We usually associate happiness and carefree days as sunny days and difficult, gloomy days as cloudy and stormy. God allows difficulties to come into our lives so that we will turn to Him for deliverance and comfort. He wants us to trust Him.

> **Is any of you in trouble? He should pray.**
> **James 5:13**

10) God sent calamity and destruction upon Egypt, bringing fear and terror to them. According to **Isaiah 19:19-22**, why did He do so? What did He want the Egyptians to do?

> **When they cry out to the Lord because of their oppressors, He will send them a savior and defender, and He will rescue them.**
> **Isaiah 19:20**

11) God allowed others to experience difficulties to capture their attention, for example Jonah, Balaam, Job, and Saul. What did God do and how did they respond? Can you think of others?

Numbers 22:21-34—

Jonah 1:17-2:10—

Acts 9:1-20—

12) What is another way God captures our attention according to **Job 33:15-22?**

> **He redeemed my soul from going down to the pit, and I will live to enjoy the light. God does all these things to a man—twice, even three times—to turn back his soul from the pit.**
> **Job 33:28-30**

> **So, the Lord will make Himself known to the Egyptians, and in that day, they will acknowledge the Lord. They will worship. . . and make vows to the Lord. . . They will turn to the Lord and He will respond to their pleas and heal them.**
> **Isaiah 19:21-22**

The Lord Almighty will bless them, saying 'Blessed be Egypt my people' (Isaiah 19:25). God loves the Egyptians and will do whatever it takes to capture their attention. He wants them to know Him, acknowledge Him, worship Him, and turn their hearts to Him.

In the same way, God loves all of us. He will do whatever it takes to capture our attention. He wants us to know Him and acknowledge Him. He wants us to worship Him. He wants us to turn our hearts to Him.

13) Describe a time in your life when God captured your attention. What did He do and how did you respond?

> **In this you greatly rejoice, though now for a little while,**

you may have had to suffer grief in all kinds of trials.
These have come so that your faith—of greater worth
than gold, which perishes even though refined by fire
—may be proved genuine and may result in praise,
glory and honor when Jesus Christ is revealed.
I Peter 1:6-7

Teach me Your way, O Lord, and I will walk in Your truth;
give me an undivided heart that I may fear Your name. I will
praise You, O Lord my God, with all my heart; I will glorify
Your name forever. For great is Your love toward me;
You have delivered me from the depths of the grave.
Psalm 86:11-13

Please read Isaiah Chapter 20.

Isaiah trusted and obeyed God, even when it meant humiliation and ridicule. When God asked Isaiah to strip and go barefoot for three years as a sign that the people will be taken away to Assyria in the same manner, Isaiah did so. In **Chapter 20** we see that the people relied on Egypt and Cush (Ethiopia) to protect them instead of calling on the Holy God of Israel.

14) What did the people realize in **verses 6**? What does the Psalmist tell us in **Psalm 33:16-17**?

The people they trusted to help them were also captured.

**It is better to take refuge in the Lord than to trust in man.
It is better to take refuge in the Lord than to trust in princes.
Psalm 118:8-9**

15) Trust is a familiar theme throughout the Bible. It seems we trust God until the next trial comes. What "horse" are you trusting in instead of God? Read aloud **Jeremiah 29:11-14**.

> At Your rebuke, O God of Jacob, both horse and chariot lie still.
> Psalm 76:6

> . . . the Lord's unfailing love surrounds
> the man who trusts in Him.
> Psalm 32:10

> We wait in hope for the Lord; He is our help and our shield. In Him our hearts rejoice, for we trust in His holy name. May Your unfailing love rest upon us, O Lord, even as we put our hope in You.
> Psalm 33:20-22

Before you go: Consider how the Lord specifically revealed Himself to you today. What words or phrases caught your attention? How do you respond to this? Lift a prayer of praise to the Lord.

Further Thoughts:

1) Where is God in verse **Isaiah 19:1**? Read the following verses. What do these images show us about God?

Deuteronomy 33:26—

Psalm 18:9-11—

Psalm 68:4—

Psalm 104:3—

2) According to **Mark 13:26, Acts 1:9-11,** and **Revelation 1:7,** who else will be found in the clouds?

3) God describes Himself as our Rock, our Fortress. Let us look at another Rock or Stone. What do we learn from the following verses? How should we respond?

Psalm 118:22-23—

Isaiah 28:16—

Matthew 21:42-44—

Acts 4:10-12—

I Peter 2:4-8—

God's Amazing Love and Faithfulness

Lesson 7: Isaiah Chapters 21-25

This week's memory verse:

> **Love the Lord your God with all your heart, and with all your soul, and with all your mind, and with all your strength.**
> **Mark 12:30**

Before you begin: Please start by praying to God. Give Him praise. Ask Him to reveal Himself and to speak to you today through this lesson.

Please read Isaiah Chapter 21.

This is a prophecy of God who releases His anger on Babylon and the surrounding countries. What is interesting is that Babylon has yet to capture Jerusalem at this time.

> **May God arise, may His enemies be scattered; may His foes flee before Him. As smoke is blown away by the wind, may You blow them away; as wax melts before the fire, may the wicked perish before God.**
> **Psalm 68:1-2.**

1) God is Sovereign and powerful. God tells of the destruction of Babylon, Edom, and Arabia with images that are horrifying. According to **Isaiah 21:3-4**, how does Isaiah respond?

Please read Isaiah Chapter 22.

And this is the prophecy that the Babylonians will capture Jerusalem. In **2 Kings Chapter 25**, we read that the people in Jerusalem were starving, the king tried to run away abandoning the people, Jerusalem and the temple were set on fire, and those who remained were taken into captivity. In the midst of God's terrible wrath, we have a glimpse of His heart. And it is broken.

Therefore I said, 'Turn away from me; let me weep bitterly. Do not try to console me over the destruction of my people.'
Isaiah 22:4

Is it Isaiah or God speaking this verse and **Isaiah 21:10**? It is possible for Isaiah to speak it. What he saw was devastating. Jeremiah, who is known as the weeping prophet interjected his thoughts and feelings throughout the prophecies. However, Isaiah only reveals his own thoughts here in **Chapters 21** and **22**. And it could be God crying out. We saw that God grieved over Moab, a neighboring country when it was captured (**Isaiah Chapters 15** and **16**). If God grieved over them, He must have grieved even more over His own people.

Please read **Isaiah 22:4** again. Can you feel the distress and passion of God? God is crying out in pain and anger! I cannot imagine God whispering these words. I imagine Him yelling out full force with thunder and lightning and everyone and everything trembling around Him!

2) To whom did God set His affection according to **Deuteronomy 7:6-9**?

God's people stole His heart. **You have stolen My heart, my sister, my bride; you have stolen My heart with one glance of your eyes, with one jewel of your necklace. How delightful** is your love, my sister, my bride! How much pleasing is your love than wine, and the fragrance of your perfume than any spice (Song of Songs 4:9-10)!

3) What did God desire from His people? See **Deuteronomy 6:4-9** and **10:12-13**.

> Place Me like a seal over your heart, like a seal on your arm; for love is as strong as death, its jealousy unyielding as the grave. It burns like blazing fire, like a mighty flame. Many waters cannot quench love; rivers cannot wash it away.
> Song of Songs 8:6-7

4) In **Deuteronomy 8:19-20**, what did God warn them? How did God's people respond to him in **verses 11-13**?

> I reared children and brought them up, but
> they have rebelled against me.
> Isaiah 1:2

> Yet they rebelled and grieved His Holy Spirit. So He turned and became their enemy and He Himself fought against them.
> Isaiah 63:10

> Anger is cruel and fury overwhelming, but
> who can stand before jealousy?
> Proverbs 27:4

> People from many nations will pass by this city and will ask one another, 'Why has the Lord done such a thing to this great city?' And the answer will be: 'Because they have forsaken the covenant of the Lord their God and have worshiped and served other gods.'
> Jeremiah 22:8-9

Israel broke God's heart. And so did we. And so do we.

Have we loved the Lord our God with all our heart and with all our soul and with all our mind and with all our strength? Do we always fear the Lord our God, walk in His ways, love Him, and serve Him with all our heart and with all our soul? Don't we disappoint and grieve God too, sometimes?

5) What does God desire from us in **Deuteronomy 10:20** and **11:22**? What does it mean to **Hold fast to Him**?

I looked for the One my heart loves; I looked for Him, but did not find Him... I will search for the one my heart loves. So I looked for Him, but did not find him. The watchmen found me as they made their rounds in the city. 'Have you seen the one My heart loves?' Scarcely had I passed them when I found the one my heart loves. I held him and would not let him go.
Song of Songs 3:1-4

My soul clings to You, Your right hand upholds me.
Psalm 63:8

He reached down from on high and took hold of me.
Psalm 18:16

But I press on to take hold of that for which Christ Jesus took hold of me.
Philippians 3:12

"The Father's longing to hold you close is
far stronger than your desire for
Him to hold you close."
Cynthia Heald, *I Have Loved You: Getting*

to Know the Father's Heart

> **Create in me a pure heart, O God, and renew a steadfast spirit within me. Do not cast me from Your presence or take Your Holy Spirit from me. Restore to me the joy of Your salvation and grant me a willing spirit to sustain me.**
> **Psalm 51:10-12**

Please read Isaiah Chapter 23.

> **The Lord will fulfill His purpose for me; Your love, O Lord endures forever—do not abandon the works of your hands.**
> **Psalm 138:8**

God's words are true. He is faithful to His Word. What He says will happen as He has planned. He has proven this many times in the past and because of this, we can depend upon His promises for our future.

6) According to **verse 9**, who planned the destruction of Tyre? And why, what was His purpose?

> **The Lord has stretched out His hand over the sea and made its kingdoms tremble. He has given an order concerning Phoenicia that her fortresses be destroyed.**
> **Isaiah 23:11**

7) What is the length of time Tyre will return (**verse 17**)? How does this compare with the prophecy regarding Judah in **Jeremiah 25:8-12** and **29:10**? What happened according to **2 Chronicles 36:20-23**?

All of God's words and promises are true. His purpose will prevail!

**Many are the plans in a man's heart, but it is
the Lord's purpose that prevails.
Proverbs 19:21**

**All Your words are true; all Your righteous laws are eternal.
Psalm 119:160**

**The Lord has done what He planned; He has fulfilled His word,
which He decreed long ago.
Lamentations 2:17**

**The ordinances of the Lord are sure and all together righteous.
They are more precious than gold, than much pure gold,
they are sweeter than honey, than honey from the comb.
Psalm 19:9-10**

8) God gives us many promises in His Word. How has God fulfilled a promise in your life?

9) What has God promised us in **2 Peter 3:13**? What does God want us to do? How do we do this (**2 Peter 3:14**)?

**For he was looking forward to the city with foundations,
whose architect and builder is God.
Hebrews 11:10**

**Instead, they were longing for a better country—
a heavenly one. Therefore, God is not ashamed to be
called their God, for He has prepared a city for them.
Hebrews 11:16**

> **Let us hold unswervingly to the hope we profess,
> for He who promised is faithful.
> Hebrews 10:23**

Please read Isaiah Chapter 24.

> **Now I saw a new heaven and a new earth, for the first heaven
> and the first earth had passed away.
> Revelation 21:1**

We have experienced God's incomprehensible love. We know that God's words are true and that He is faithful to His promises. We have seen His promises fulfilled and can trust that His promises will continue to be fulfilled in the future. But these words are frightening! God is going to destroy the heavens and the earth?! Why does a loving God want to destroy His creation? What does this tell us about God and what does all of this mean for us?

10) Look up the following verses. What did God promise in His Word about this earth?

Deuteronomy 32:22—

Zephaniah 1:2-3, 14-18—

Matthew 24:29, 35—

2 Peter 3:7, 10, 12—

11) According to **verse 5**, why is God going to destroy the earth? What more can we learn from **Psalm 58:10-11** and **Psalm 79:6**?

> **How great are Your works, O Lord, how profound Your**

> thoughts! The senseless man does not know, fools do not understand. That though the wicked spring up like grass and all evildoers flourish, they will be forever destroyed... For surely Your enemies, O Lord, surely Your enemies will perish; all evildoers will be scattered.
> **Psalm 92:5-9**

12) What right does God have for doing this? Use **Genesis 1:1** and **Psalm 89:11** to help you answer.

13) What does Jesus say was His purpose for coming in **Luke 12:49**? What do **Hebrews 2:14** and **I John 3:8** tell us of Jesus' purpose?

> I have told you these things, so that in Me you may have peace. In this world you will have trouble. But take heart! I have overcome the world.
> **John 16:33**

14) What hope do we find in this chapter (**verse 23**)? What additional hope can we find in these verses?

Joel 2:32—

Romans 8:18-25—

Revelation 21:1-4—

> For God so loved the world that He gave His one and only Son, that whoever believes in Him shall not perish, but have eternal life.
> **John 3:16**

> **If you make the Most High your dwelling—even the Lord, who is my refuge--then no harm will befall you, no disaster will come near your tent.**
> **Psalm 91:9-10**

Please read Isaiah Chapter 25.

As we learned in **Isaiah chapter 1**, God already has a plan for His creation, for His people and for this world. And it is all for His glory and honor. What is so amazing is that He has planned every tiny detail, including the details of your life. He has taken care of you so far. Doesn't it cause you to wonder what He has already planned for your future? He has proven Himself to be faithful to His promises, so we can trust Him to be true. We can give Him the honor and praise He deserves.

> **O Lord, you are my God; I will exalt You and praise Your Name, for in perfect faithfulness you have done marvelous things, things planned long ago.**
> **Isaiah 25:1**

15) What wonderful and marvelous things has the Lord done in your life?

> **Many, O Lord my God are the wonders You have done. The things You planned for us no one can recount to You; were I to speak and tell of them, they would be too many to declare.**
> **Psalm 40:5**

> **All the days ordained for me were written in Your book before one of them came to be. How precious to me are Your thoughts, O God! How vast is the sum of them! Were I to count them, they would outnumber the grains of sand.**
> **Psalm 139:16-18**

> **You are worthy, our Lord and God, to receive glory and honor and power, for You created all things, and by Your will they were created and have their being.**
> **Revelation 4:11**

16) What is God's promise for us in **verse 6**? What does Jesus teach us about this event in the following verses?

Matthew 8:11—

Matthew 25:1-10—

Matthew 26:29—

> **You prepare a table before me in the presence of my enemies.**
> **Psalm 23:5**

> **My soul will be satisfied with the richest of foods.**
> **Psalm 63:5**

17) What does the shroud or covering represent that God will destroy in **verses 7-8**? Consider the following verses to help with your answer: **Isaiah 26:19, I Corinthians 15:20-26**, and **Hebrews 2:14-15**.

> **There will be no more death, or mourning or crying or pain, for the old order of things has passed away.**
> **Revelation 21:4**

> **But God will redeem my life from the grave;**
> **He will surely take me to Himself.**
> **Psalm 49:15**

> **Surely this is our God; we trusted in Him and He**

saved us. This is the Lord, we trusted in Him; let us rejoice and be glad in His salvation.
Isaiah 25:9

Let us rejoice and be glad in His salvation!

So, Christ was sacrificed once to take away the sins of many people and He will appear a second time, not to bear sin, but to bring salvation to those who are waiting for Him.
Hebrews 9:28

Praise be to the God and Father of our Lord Jesus Christ! In His great mercy He has given us new birth into a living hope through the resurrection of Jesus Christ from the dead, and into an inheritance that can never perish, spoil or fade—kept in heaven for you, who through faith are shielded by God's power until the coming of the salvation that is ready to be revealed in the last time.
1 Peter 1:3-5

Before you go: Consider how the Lord specifically revealed Himself to you today. What words or phrases caught your attention? How do you respond to this? Lift a prayer of praise to the Lord.

Further Thoughts:

God does all these marvelous things in His faithfulness. Let us look deeper at God's faithfulness. It is one of His characteristics, one of the fruits of the Holy Spirit (see **Galatians 5:22**) and the name of Jesus Christ (**Revelation 19:11**). To whom is He faithful? How does He show His faithfulness? How enduring is His faithfulness? What do the following verses teach us about God's faithfulness?

Deuteronomy 7:9—

Psalm 89:2—

Romans 3:3-4—

2 Thessalonians 3:3—

Hebrews 10:23—

I John 1:9—

> **Because of the Lord's great love, we are not consumed, for His compassions never fail.**

**They are new every morning; great is Your faithfulness.
Lamentations 3:22-23**

God of Peace, A Beautiful Crown, The Holy One

Lesson 8: Isaiah Chapters 26-29

This week's memory verse:

> **You will keep in perfect peace him whose mind is steadfast, because he trusts in You.**
> **Isaiah 26:3**

Before you begin: Please start by praying to God. Give Him praise. Ask Him to reveal Himself and to speak to you today through this lesson.

Please read Isaiah Chapter 26.

When distressing circumstances surround us, we can find peace in God by trusting in Him alone and looking forward to our future with Him in heaven. Let us look more intently on the God of Peace as He reveals Himself in this chapter.

1) Read **verse 1**. What does a strong city imply for those who dwell within it? What are the walls of this city made of? Who is the builder of this city? What city is described here? What do the following verses tell us about this city: **Psalm 48:1-3** and **Revelation 21:10-14; 26-27**?

2) What is the name of God in **verse 7**? What does He do for us?

    a) What might be in our path to make us stumble?

Consider **Matthew 14:28-30, Luke 8:13-15,** and **1 John 2:9-10**.

b) What do these verses teach us to keep from stumbling? **Psalm 37:23-24, Psalm 94:18, Psalm 119:165, Proverbs 3:5-6,** and **Proverbs 4:10-27**.

> **Therefore, since we are surrounded by such a great cloud of witnesses, let us throw off everything that hinders and the sin that so easily entangles, and let us run with perseverance the race marked out for us. Let us fix our eyes of Jesus, the author and perfecter of our faith.**
> **Hebrews 12:1-2**

3) What does God desire in **verses 8-9**? What does He want us to do? Read **Psalm 84:2**. Have you ever longed or yearned for the Lord? If so, describe the circumstances and how you felt. How did God respond?

> **Acknowledge the God of your Father, and serve Him with wholehearted devotion and with a willing mind... If you seek Him, He will be found by you.**
> **1 Chronicles 28:9**

4) What has God given us in **verse 12**? What does God promise in **Ezekiel 37: 24-27** and **Micah 5:4-5**? What does Jesus tell us about himself in **John 14:27**?

5) How can we experience this peace according to **verses 3-4**?

> **Do not be anxious about anything, but in everything,
> by prayer and petition, with thanksgiving, present
> your requests to God. And the peace of God,
> which transcends all understanding, will guard
> your hearts and minds in Christ Jesus.
> Philippians 4:6-7**

6) What hope and promise do we find in **verse 19**? What happened in **Matthew 27:52-53**?

7) What assurances do we find in **1 Corinthians 15:51-57** and **1 Thessalonians 4:13-17**?

Please read Isaiah Chapter 27.

8) Here God continues to tell us about end times. **"In that day. . ."** Compare **verse 1** with **Revelation 19:19-21**. The evil in this world will be destroyed. After reading this, what do we learn about God?

9) In **Isaiah Chapter 5** we learned that the vineyard is Israel, God's people. What do we see God doing in **verses 2-5**? What does He long for in **verse 5**?

> **The Lord looks down from heaven on the sons of men to
> see if there are any who understand, any who seek God.
> Psalm 14:2**

> **Therefore, since we have been justified through faith, we have peace with God through our Lord Jesus Christ.**
> **Romans 5:1**

God ends this Chapter with a glorious promise! The Lord has established peace for us, and we will worship Him.

> **At that time the sign of the Son of Man will appear in the sky. . . and He will send His angels with a loud trumpet call, and they will gather His elect from the four winds, from the end of the heavens to the other.**
> **Matthew 24:30-31**

> **(They) will come and worship the Lord on the holy mountain in Jerusalem.**
> **Isaiah 27:13**

> **Shout for joy to the Lord, all the earth. Worship the Lord with gladness; come before Him with joyful songs.**
> **Psalm 100:1-2**

> **Find rest, O my soul, in God alone; my hope comes from Him. He alone is my rock and my salvation; He is my fortress; I will not be shaken. My salvation and my honor depend on God; He is my mighty rock, my refuge. Trust in Him at all times, O people; pour out your hearts to Him, for God is our refuge.**
> **Psalm 62:5-8**

Please read Isaiah Chapter 28.

Picture a beautiful crown, rich in jewels. A crown or wreath represents glory and honor. The bearer is given the right to rule and to judge. God is the Supreme Wise Judge, who has the authority to condemn or set free.

10) How is Ephraim described in **verse 1**? What is he wearing? What happens to Ephraim in **verses 2-4**?

11) How is the Lord described in **verses 5-6**? What does this mean?

> **This is what the Lord says: 'Let not the wise man boast of his wisdom or the strong may boast of his strength or the rich man boast of his riches, but let him who boast, boast about this: that he understands and knows me, that I am the Lord, who exercises kindness, justice and righteousness on earth, for in these I delight,' declares the Lord.**
> **Jeremiah 9:23-24**

> **The Lord reigns forever; He has established His throne for judgment. He will judge the world in righteousness; He will govern the peoples with justice.**
> **Psalm 9:7-8**

12) What is Jesus wearing in the following verses?

Matthew 27:28-29—

Hebrews 2:9—

Revelation 14:14—

Revelation 19:11-12—

13) What does God want us to be filled with instead of wine according to **Ephesians 5:18**? What do we learn from **Romans 8:9-11**?

Like God's people in **verses 9-13**, sometimes as believers, we too get caught up in rules and traditions, in doing good and serving to the point of forgetting who we are serving. God knows that it is impossible for us to be perfect. **For all have sinned and fall short of the glory of God. Romans 3:23.** Paul also describes his exacerbation in **Romans 7:14-25**.

14) What hope do we find in **Romans 3:21-22** and **Romans 5:1, 20-21**? What does **Hebrews 10:1-18** teach us?

> **Therefore, there is now no condemnation for those who are in Christ Jesus because through Christ Jesus the law of the Spirit of Life set me free from the law of sin and death.**
> **Romans 8:1-2**

> **Christ is the mediator of a new covenant, that those who are called may receive the promised eternal inheritance —now that He has died as a ransom to set them free from the sins committed under the first covenant.**
> **Hebrews 9:15**

15) How is God described in **verse 29**? How does God show His magnificent wisdom?

> **For the Lord gives wisdom and from His mouth come knowledge and understanding. He holds victory in store for the upright., He is a shield to those whose walk is blameless, for He guards the course of the just and protects the way of His faithful ones.**
> **Proverbs 2:6-8**

Please read Isaiah Chapter 29.

> **Our Father in heaven, hallowed be Your Name.**
> **Matthew 6:9**

In this chapter, Almighty God again shows His power. We may think that God does not see us and that we can hide our sin from Him, but He sees our true heart. He rebukes our false worship. He desires our full devotion and reverence.

16) In **verses 1-4**, God again tells His people that they will be overcome by their enemies. But what happens in **verses 5-8**? How is God described in **verse 6**? How does this compare with **Psalm 18:7-15**?

> **But the Lord is the true God; He is the Living God, the Eternal King. When He is angry, the earth trembles; the nations cannot endure His wrath.**
> **Jeremiah 10:10**

17) What is God's desire in **verses 13-14**? What can we learn from the following verses?

Proverbs 15:8—

Ecclesiastes 5:1-2—

Hosea 6:6—

Mark 12:33—

John 4:24—

> **Woe to those who go to great depths to hide their**

> plans from the Lord, who do their work in darkness
> and think, 'Who sees us? Who will know?'
> Isaiah 29:15

18) We are foolish to think we can hide from God. What do these verses remind us about God?

Job 34:21-22—

Psalm 139:1-12—

Ecclesiastes 12:14—

Romans 2:16—

Hebrews 4:13—

19) How is **verse 16** like the beliefs in our world today?

> Yet, O Lord, You are our Father. We are
> the clay; You are the potter;
> we are all the work of Your hand.
> Isaiah 64:8

20) How is God described in **verse 23**? What does He want?

> May my prayer be set before You like incense;
> may the lifting up of my hands
> be like the evening sacrifice.
> Psalm 141:2

The Lord reigns, let the nations tremble; He sits enthroned

between the cherubim, let the earth shake. Great is the Lord in Zion, He is exalted over all the nations. Let them praise Your great and awesome name—He is holy.
Psalm 99:1-3

Before you go: Consider how the Lord specifically revealed Himself to you today. What words or phrases caught your attention? How do you respond to this? Lift a prayer of praise to the Lord.

Digging Deeper:

1) In **Isaiah 28:5**, God is described as a Crown of Glory. What is Jesus wearing in the following verses? What does this represent?

Matthew 27:28-29—

Hebrews 2:9—

Revelation 14:14—

Revelation 19:11-12—

2) God was angry with the people who honored Him with their lips only and not with their heart (**Isaiah 29:13**). What do the following verses teach us about true worship?

Proverbs 15:8—

Ecclesiastes 5:1-2—

Hosea 6:6—

Mark 12:33—

Our Righteous God Who Answers

Lesson 9: Isaiah Chapters 30-32

This week's memory verse:

> **I seek You with all my heart; do not let me stray from Your commands.**
> **I have hidden Your Word in my heart that I might not sin against You.**
> **Psalm 119:10-11**

Before you begin: Please start by praying to God. Give Him praise. Ask Him to reveal Himself and to speak to you today through this lesson.

God's people are obstinate! They continue to look to idols and in this chapter, they look to Egypt for help instead of calling out to God. God longs to be gracious to His people. If they would cry out to Him, He says He will answer them. And He longs to do the same for us.

Please read Isaiah Chapter 30.

1) What are some of the things that upset God in verses **1-17**?

2) According to the following verses, what does God want us to do instead? What does He promise us?

I Chronicles 28:9—

Isaiah 55:6—

Matthew 6:33—

Matthew 7:7-11—

3) Using a dictionary, define the word **Repent**. In **verse 15**, what does God desire from us?

    As believers, when we sin against God, and we cannot rest until we confess our wrongdoing and turn away from our sin.

> **In repentance and rest is your salvation, in**
> **quietness and trust is your strength.**
> **Isaiah 30:15**

> **Turn to me and be gracious to me, for I am lonely and afflicted.**
> **The troubles of my heart have multiplied;**
> **free me from my anguish.**
> **Look upon my affliction and my distress**
> **and take away all my sins.**
> **Psalm 25:16-18**

> **Repent, then, and turn to God, so that**
> **your sins may be wiped out,**
> **that times of refreshing may come from the Lord.**
> **Acts 3:19**

4) What does God tell us about Himself in **verses 18-21**? What does He want to do for us? How does He respond to our cries of help? How does **Psalm 116:1-7** complement these verses?

> **The Lord is near to all who call on Him, to**
> **all who call on Him in truth.**

> **He fulfills the desires of those who fear him;**
> **He hears their cry and saves them.**
> **Psalm 145:18-19**

5) Jesus also shows compassion in **Matthew 15:32-37** and **Matthew 20:29-34**. How did He respond to their distress?

6) It is common in Isaiah for prophecies to have double meaning. **Verses 27-33** are a prophecy of the destruction of Assyria and of the end times. God shows His power and vengeance against our enemies and their end result. Compare these verses to **Revelation 19:11-21**.

During the time of Isaiah, the northern kingdom, Israel, was captured by the Assyrians. Jerusalem and Judah were protected by God. God assures His people that their oppressor, the Assyrians, will be destroyed. It will be years later after Isaiah's time, before the Babylonians overpower the Assyrians and destroy Jerusalem. Let us look to see how God reveals Himself in the next chapter.

Please read Isaiah Chapter 31.

7) How does God describe Himself in **verse 2**? What do the following verses tell us about God?

God is wise: **Psalm 104:24** and **Proverbs 2:6**.

God is faithful. He does not take back His word: **Psalm 18:30, Isaiah 55:11**, and **Matthew 24:35**.

God is powerful. He will rise up against His enemiies: **Psalm 66:3** and **147:5**

8) How is God described in **verse 5**? What does He do for Jerusalem? Describe a time when God was a shield, a protector for you.

> **But You are a shield around me, O Lord.**
> **Psalm 3:3**
>
> **For surely, O Lord, You bless the righteous;**
> **You surround them with Your favor as with a shield.**
> **Psalm 5:12**
>
> **He will cover you with His feathers, and under**
> **His wings you will find refuge;**
> **His faithfulness will be your shield and rampart.**
> **Psalm 91:4**

9) What does God desire of His people in **verse 6**? He is not a tyrant who demands that we return to Him out of fear. He is a loving, compassionate God whom we cannot help but run back to when we have strayed. How do the following verses show God's love?

2 Chronicles 30:6-9—

Jeremiah 24:6-7—

Hosea 6:1-3—

Luke 15:11-24—

> Let us examine our ways and test them,
> and let us return to the Lord.
> Let us lift up our hearts and our hands
> to God in heaven and say:
> "We have sinned and rebelled..."
> **Lamentations 3:40-42**

> I have strayed like a lost sheep. Seek Your servant, for I have not forgotten Your commands. Before I was afflicted, I went astray, but now I obey Your word. Turn my eyes away from worthless things; preserve my life according to Your word. I recounted my ways, and You answered me; teach me Your decrees. I seek You will all my heart; do not let me stray from Your commands. I have sought Your face with all my heart; be gracious to me according to Your promise. Let Your compassion come to me that I may live, for Your law is my delight.
> From **Psalm 119**

Please read Isaiah Chapter 32.

This is a prophecy of the Messiah, Jesus Christ, the Savior. The Messiah, the King of Righteousness will reign over a kingdom of peace and security. Injustice and evil brings only chaos and oppression, but where there is justice and righteousness, there is peace. The wicked and foolish will not live there. Nor will anyone who is complacent, who does not put his hope in Christ.

10) **Verse 1** tells us of the Messiah King. How do the following verses describe the Messiah?

Psalm 45:2-7—

Isaiah 9:7—

Isaiah 16:5—

Hebrews 1:8-9—

Hebrews 6:20-7:2—

> **The Lord has sworn and will not change His mind: "You are a priest forever, In the order of Melchizedek."**
> **Psalm 110:4**

11) Compare **verses 3-4** with **I Corinthians 13:9-12** and **I John 3:2**. What do we learn about ourselves in this future heavenly kingdom?

12) According to **verses 9-14** and **Deuteronomy 32:13-15**, what can happen when we are satisfied and have everything we need?

> **Find rest, O my soul, in God alone, my hope comes from Him.**
> **He alone is my rock and my salvation; He is**
> **my fortress. I will not be shaken.**

Psalm 62-5-6

13) What are the benefits of righteousness according to **verses 16-20**?

Our world will continue to have its struggles and distress as long as sin rules. However, if we choose to live righteous lives, we too can **live in peaceful dwelling places, in secure homes and in undisturbed places of rest (verse 18).**

> **But as for me, I will always have hope; I**
> **will praise You more and more.**
> **My mouth will tell of Your righteousness,**
> **of Your salvation all day long,**
> **Though I know not its measure.**
> **Psalm 71:14-15**

Before you go: Consider how the Lord specifically revealed Himself to you today. What words or phrases caught your attention? How do you respond to this? Lift a prayer of praise to the Lord.

Further Thoughts:

Our God is righteous, wise, faithful, and powerful. He wants us to repent and turn to Him. He already knows our struggles and concerns, and He knows best how to help us.

1) Describe a time when God was either righteous, wise, faithful, or powerful in your life.

2) What can we do to live righteous lives?

And I—in righteousness I will see Your face; when I awake, I will be satisfied with seeing Your likeness.
Psalm 17:15

Our Beautiful, Glorious God
Lesson 10: Isaiah Chapters 33-35

This week's memory verse:

> **And the ransomed of the Lord will return.**
> **They will enter Zion with singing;**
> **everlasting joy will crown their heads. Gladness**
> **and joy will overtake them,**
> **and sorrow and sighing will flee away.**
> **Isaiah 35:10**

Before you begin: Please start by praying to God. Give Him praise. Ask Him to reveal Himself and to speak to you today through this lesson.

Please read Isaiah Chapter 33.

1) Assyria has captured the northern kingdom and the people in Jerusalem are distressed and worried about what will happen to them. What do the people cry out in **verse 2**?

> **In the morning O Lord, You hear my voice; in the morning**
> **I lay my requests before You and wait in expectation.**
> **Psalm 5:3**

2) How is God described in **verses 5** and **10**?

Exalt means "to hold someone or something in very high regard; think or speak very highly of. Raise to a higher rank or a position of greater power" (The New Oxford American Dictionary).

3) How can we exalt our Lord daily?

> **I will extol the Lord at all times, His praise will always be on my lips... Glorify the Lord with me, let us exalt His Name together.**
> **Psalm 34:1-3**

> **He will be the sure foundation for your times, a rich store of salvation and wisdom and knowledge; the fear of the Lord is the key to this treasure.**
> **Isaiah 33:6**

4) God is our sure foundation, our stability, our strength. He gives us wisdom and knowledge. He also strengthens our hope. How does **Ephesians 2:19-22** define God's foundation? What does **verse 6** tell us is the key to this treasure?

> **We have this hope as an anchor for the soul, firm and secure.**
> **Hebrews 6:19**

> **The fear of the Lord is the beginning of wisdom.**
> **Psalm 111:10**

5) How is God described in **verse 17**? What about our Lord is beautiful to you?

> **One thing I ask of the Lord, this is what I seek: that I may dwell in the house of the Lord all the days of my life, to gaze upon the beauty of the Lord and to seek Him in His temple.**
> **Psalm 27:4**

6) In **verse 22** God describes Himself as Judge and Lawgiver. But He also is described as our King and Savior who knows that we falter and sin against Him. If He were to judge us as we are, we would be condemned. Praise God that in His perfect love He is also our King and Savior! In **verse 24**, what is the promise to those who dwell in Zion?

> **Blessed is he whose transgressions are forgiven, whose sins are covered. Blessed is the man whose sin the Lord does not count against him and in whose spirit is no deceit.**
> **Psalm 32:1-2**

> **O Lord, be gracious to us; we long for You. Be our strength every morning, our salvation in times of distress.**
> **Isaiah 33:2**

Please read Isaiah Chapter 34.

This chapter again describes the destruction of the evil in this world and its final end as God displays His anger and wrath. But the first verse reminds us of His love. He created this beautiful perfect world and Satan tainted it. God loves all of the people He created. If only they would come to Him and listen!

7) What is God's plea in **verse 1**?

8) What do the following verses teach us? What might prevent us from hearing God?

Deuteronomy 30:19-20—

I Kings 19:11-13—

Mark 9:7—

John 10:2-5, 27—

James 1:22-25—

> **Whether you turn to the right or to the left, your ears will hear a voice behind you, saying, "This is the way; walk in it."**
> **Isaiah 30:21**

> **Today, if you hear His voice, do not harden your hearts...**
> **Psalm 95:7-8**

9) Let us pause for a moment and think about the horrors of this world. Doesn't it sicken and anger you? How is God described in **verses 2** and **8**? He will take vengeance against evil! How does this chapter compare with **Psalm 10**?

> **For the Lord will vindicate His people and**
> **have compassion on His servants.**
> **Psalm 135:14**

> **God is our refuge and strength, an ever-present help in trouble. Therefore we will not fear, though the earth give way and the mountains fall into the heart of the sea, though its waters roar and foam and the mountains quake with their surging... Nations are in uproar, kingdoms fall; He lifts His voice, the earth melts... Come and see the works of the Lord, the desolations He has brought on the earth. He makes wars cease to the ends of the earth; He breaks the bow and shatters the spear; He burns the shields with fire. Be still, and know that I am God; I will be exalted among the nations, I will be exalted in the earth...**
> **Psalm 46**

Please read Isaiah Chapter 35.

After God destroys all evil, He will take us to our new home. What will the new heavens and the earth be like? This chapter gives us a little glimpse!

10) What happened to nature when sin entered the world in **Genesis 3:17-18?**

> **The land mourns and wastes away, Lebanon is ashamed and withers.**
> **Isaiah 33:9**

11) How is nature described in this chapter? What will all of nature see, according to **verse 2?** How does **Psalm 148** exemplify this?

12) What is promised in verses **3-6?** What do we see Jesus doing in the following verses?

Matthew 9:1-8—

Matthew 12:22—

Luke 7:21-22—

> **And a highway will be there; it will be called the Way of Holiness... it will be for those who walk in the Way... But only the redeemed will walk there.**
> **Isaiah 35:8-9**

13) What does Jesus proclaim in **John 14:6?** What do the new believers call themselves in **Acts 22:4?** Who only is allowed to

walk on this highway?

> **He led them by a straight way to a city where they could settle.**
> **Psalm 107:7**

> **For here we do not have an enduring city,**
> **but we are looking forward for the city that is to come.**
> **Hebrews 13:14**

14) **Psalm 126** describes how the captives felt when they returned to Zion. How will we respond when we enter the new Jerusalem, into the presence of God (**verse 10**)?

> **Send forth Your light and Your truth, let them guide me; let them bring me to Your Holy Mountain, to the place where You dwell. Then I will go to the alter of God, to God, my joy and my delight. I will praise You with the harp, O God, my God.**
> **Psalm 43:3-4**

> **Clap your hands, all you nations; shout to God with cries of joy. How awesome is the Lord Most High, the great King over all the earth!**
> **Psalm 47:1-2**

Before you go: Consider how the Lord specifically revealed Himself to you today. What words or phrases caught your attention? How do you respond to this? Lift a prayer of praise to the Lord.

Further Thoughts:

In **Isaiah Chapter 33:5, 10**, God is described as being exalted. How is Jesus described in the following verses?

John 3:14-15—

John 8:28—

John 12:32—

Acts 2:32-33—

Acts 5:30-31—

Ephesians 1:19-23—

Philippians 2:9—

Hebrews 7:26—

The Fulfillment

Lesson 11: Isaiah Chapters 36-39

This week's memory verse:

The Lord has done what He planned; He has fulfilled His word, which He decreed long ago.
Lamentations 2:17

Before you begin: Please start by praying to God. Give Him praise. Ask Him to reveal Himself and to speak to you today through this lesson.

These next few chapters remind us that Isaiah was a real person who lived during the reign of King Hezekiah. You can also find these chapters almost verbatim in **2 Kings Chapters 18-20**. King Hezekiah was a good king who enjoyed a close relationship with God. Two of his prayers to God are recorded here. We hear King Hezekiah's pleas, and we see God's tender mercy toward him as He answers King Hezekiah's prayers. God's tender mercy extends to us as well.

At this time, Sennacherib, King of Assyria has captured and destroyed the northern kingdom of Israel. God's warnings and prophecies came true. Sennacherib hopes to capture Jerusalem, but God has other plans.

Please read Isaiah Chapters 36-37.

1) What happened in **Isaiah 36:1**? Who gave him authority to do so according to **verse 10**?

> **Have you not heard? Long ago I ordained
> it, in days of old I planned it;
> now I have brought it to pass.**
> **Isaiah 37:26**

2) What did God promise would happen in **Deuteronomy 8:19-20**? What did God prophecy in **Isaiah 8:5-8** and **9:8-21**?

3) How did King Hezekiah respond to the news according to **Isaiah 37:1** and **14-20**?

4) What does Jesus teach us in **Luke 11:5-10**? Can you think of examples in Scripture when God planned something, but seemingly allowed Himself to be persuaded by man?

> **The eyes of the Lord are on the righteous and
> His ears are attentive to their prayer.**
> **I Peter 3:12**

5) How did God respond to King Hezekiah's prayer (**verses 33-39**)?

With God's authority, the Assyrians attacked, destroyed, and captured God's people in Israel, the northern kingdom. Because King Hezekiah humbled himself before the Lord, he and the people of Jerusalem (Judah, the southern kingdom) were spared—for a time.

> **Your Word, O Lord, is eternal; it stands firm in the heavens.**
> **Psalm 119:89**

Please read Isaiah Chapters 38.

Again, God, with His deep compassion, seemingly allows Himself to be persuaded by man. God prophesied through Isaiah that King Hezekiah was going to die. God not only answered his prayer and extended his life, but also assured him with an amazing miracle.

6) How did God show His compassion in **verses 1-5**?

7) How does God display His compassion and power in **verses 7-8**? How does God answer Joshua's prayer in **Joshua 10:12-14**?

> **Have you ever given orders to the morning or shown the dawn its place? ... What is the way to the abode of light? And where does darkness reside? Can you take them to their places? Do you know the paths to their dwellings?**
> **Job 38:12, 19-20**

8) What did God do for King Hezekiah in **verse 17**? How does God show His tender mercy to us in **Psalm 103:11-12** and **Micah 7:18-19**?

> **Repent, then, and turn to God, so that your sins may be wiped out, that times of refreshing may come from the Lord.**
> **Acts 3:19**

9) God has shown His compassion many times in His Word. Jesus also showed the compassion of the Father. Look up the following verses. What evidence do we find of God's tender mercy and compassion? Can you think of other examples in Scripture?

Genesis 21:9-20—

I Samuel 1:1-20—

Luke 5:12-13—

Luke 7:11-15—

> This is the confidence we have in approaching God: that if we ask anything according to His will, He hears us. And if we know that He hears us—whatever we ask—we know that we have what we asked of Him."
> **I John 5:14-15**

10) Describe a time when God showed His tender mercy and compassion to you.

Please read Isaiah Chapter 39.

King Hezekiah was a good king, but he was not perfect. He had a problem with pride. During a visit of Babylonian officials, King Hezekiah gladly displayed his wealth to them. And his prideful actions had devastating consequences.

11) What did King Hezekiah do in **verse 2**? How did God respond to this in **verses 5-7**? What happened in **2 Kings 24:8-15**?

> Pride goes before destruction and a haughty spirit before a fall.
> **Proverbs 16:18**

He has shown you O man, what is good. And

> **what does the Lord require of you?**
> **To act justly and to love mercy and to**
> **walk humbly with your God.**
> **Micah 6:8**

God fulfilled His prophecies. The Babylonians captured Jerusalem.
2 Kings Chapter 25 describes this event.

> **It was because of the Lord's anger that all this**
> **happened to Jerusalem and Judah, and in the**
> **end, He thrust them from His presence.**
> **2 Kings 24:20**

12) God's people cried out to God in **Psalm 79** and **Lamentations 5**. Describe their despair.

> **Restore us, O God, make Your face shine**
> **upon us, that we may be saved.**
> **Psalm 80:3**

Before you go: Consider how the Lord specifically revealed Himself to you today. What words or phrases caught your attention? How do you respond to this? Lift a prayer of praise to the Lord.

Further Thoughts:

1) If God is true and faithful to His word, how do we explain when it seems like He changes His mind and is persuaded by

man's pleas? Use Scripture to support your answer.

2) Can you think of a time when you cried out to God and He answered your prayer, changing your circumstances?

Our Shepherd, Our Servant

Lesson 12: Isaiah Chapters 40-42

This week's memory verse:

> **He tends His flock like a shepherd: He gathers the lambs in His arms and carries them close to His heart; He gently leads those that have young.**
> **Isaiah 40:11**

Before you begin: Please start by praying to God. Give Him praise. Ask Him to reveal Himself and to speak to you today through this lesson.

In the first part of Isaiah God warned His people of the upcoming destruction caused by their sins. In the rest of Isaiah, God gives His assurances and promises to His people. They will be forgiven of their sins and will return to Zion. And He also assures and promises us that we too will be forgiven and will enter into Zion, our heavenly home, if we accept His gift of salvation.

> **My people have been lost sheep; their shepherds have led them astray and caused them to roam on the mountains. They wandered over mountain and hill and forgot their own resting place. Whoever found them devoured them; their enemies said, "We are not guilty, for they sinned against the Lord, their true pasture, the Lord, the hope of their fathers."**
> **Jeremiah 50:6-7**

Please read Isaiah Chapter 40.

1) How does God express His heart in **verses 1-2**? Describe a time when God comforted you. What encouragement do we find in **2 Corinthians 4:8-9** and **16-17**?

> **Praise be to the God and Father of our Lord Jesus Christ, the Father of compassion and the God of all comfort, who comforts us in all our troubles so that we can comfort those in any trouble with the comfort we ourselves have received from God.**
> **2 Corinthians 1:3-4**

2) According to **Luke 3:2-6** and **John 1:23**, who is this voice (**verse 3**)? What was His purpose (**John 1:6-7**)?

> **And the glory of the Lord will be revealed, and all mankind together will see it.**
> **Isaiah 40:5**

> **The Word became flesh and made His dwelling among us. We have seen His glory, the glory of the One and Only, who came from the Father, full of grace and truth.**
> **John 1:14**

3) What assurance do we find in **verse 8**? **John 1:1-2** tells us that Jesus Christ is the Word of God. What characteristic of God do we find here and in the following verses: **Psalm 90:2; 93:2**, and **145:13**?

> **Jesus Christ is the same yesterday and today and forever.**
> **Hebrews 13:8**

4) How is God described in **verse 10**? What does He bring with

Him? What do **Jude 14-15** and **Revelation 22:12** tell us about this event?

> **And now, dear children, continue in Him, so that when He appears we may be confident and unashamed before His coming.**
> **I John 2:28**

5) How is God described in **verse 11**? What actions do you see Him doing? What do we learn about our Shepherd King in the following verses?

Psalm 23:1-4—

Ezekiel 34:11-16, 23-24—

Luke 15:3-7—

John 10:11-15—

> **For He is our God, and we are the people of His pasture, the flock under His care.**
> **Psalm 95:7**

God shows His love and compassion to His people. He comforts them and calls them back to Him. Yet the rest of the chapter shows God presenting His case before His people, the people who sought other gods and other countries for help. He challenges their disbelief by showing His sovereign authority and power.

6) What sovereign authority and power does God present in the rest of this chapter?

7) What does God promise to those who hope in Him (**verses 29-31**)?

> "In those days, at that time," declares the Lord, "the people of Israel and the people of Judah together will go in tears to seek the Lord their God. They will ask the way to Zion and turn their faces toward it. They will come and bind themselves to the Lord in an everlasting covenant that will not be forgotten."
> Jeremiah 50:4-5

> He will stand and shepherd His flock in the strength of the Lord, in the majesty of the name of the Lord His God. And they will live securely, for then His greatness will reach to the ends of the earth. And He will be their peace.
> Micah 5:4-5

> For the Lamb at the center of the throne will be their shepherd; He will lead them to springs of living water.
> Revelation 7:17

Please read Isaiah Chapter 41.

> Be still before the Lord, all mankind; because He has roused Himself from His Holy dwelling.
> Zechariah 3:13

> The Lord is in His Holy Temple; let all the earth be silent before Him.
> Habakkuk 2:20

8) What does it mean to be silent before the Lord?

We are in a courtroom where God challenges His enemies and the false gods of the nations. And they have been found wanting. God is superior. He has prevailed. No man and no idol can do what He can do because He is the Lord, the Holy One of Israel. He is eternal. He was with us from the beginning and will be with us until the end. He is all-powerful and will defeat His enemies. Throughout this defense, God gives us many assurances and promises. Let us look at what He wants to do for us.

> **Who has done this and carried it through, calling forth the generations from the beginning? I, the Lord— with the first of them and with the last—I am He.**
> **Isaiah 41:4**

> **I took you from the ends of the earth, from its farthest corners I called you.**
> **I said, "You are my servant;" I have chosen you and have not rejected you.**
> **Isaiah 41:9**

9) Record what God says He will do for us in the following verses:

Verse 10—

Verses 11-12—

Verse 13—

Verse 14—

Verse 17—

10) Note that in **verse 10** God holds you with His right hand, so He is on our left side. And in **verse 13**, He takes hold of your right hand, so He is on our right side. Look up the following verses and note where God is located in relation to us:

Deuteronomy 31:8—

Deuteronomy 33:12, 27—

Psalm 125:2—

Psalm 139:5; 7-10—

John 17:21-23—

Acts 17:28—

> I am always with You; You hold me by my right hand. You guide me with Your counsel, and afterward You will take me into glory. Whom have I in heaven but You? And earth has nothing I desire besides You.
> Psalm 73:23-25

> The Lord is gracious and compassionate;
> slow to anger and rich in love.
> The Lord is good to all; He has compassion on all He has made.
> Psalm 145:8-9

Please read Isaiah Chapter 42.

In this chapter, God gives us the first of four prophecies of the Messiah Servant. Note that in the NKJV "Servant" is capitalized, meaning this is not a servant but **the** Servant, one of significance. In **verse 8** God says **I am the Lord; that is my name! I will not give my glory to another** . . . indicating that this Servant is Himself, His Chosen One, the Messiah, His Son Jesus Christ. Only Jesus Christ is glorified with God, because the two are one.

> **Jesus said, "Now is the Son of Man glorified and God is glorified in Him."**
> **John 13:31**

11) In what ways does Jesus fulfill the prophecy of the Messiah Servant in **verses 1-9**? Consider the following verses as you answer:

Matthew 3:16-17—

Matthew 11:5—

Matthew 12:15-21—

Acts 13:47-48—

Hebrews 9:15—

12) How are God's people blind and deaf according to **verses 18-25**? How did God attempt to capture their attention in **verses 24-25**?

> **Again, I ask: Did they stumble so as to fall beyond recovery? Not at all! Rather, because of their transgression, salvation has come to the Gentiles to make Israel**

> envious. But if their transgression means riches for
> the world, and their loss means riches for the Gentiles,
> how much greater riches will their fullness bring!
> **Romans 11:11-12**

13) What does God promise us in **verses 7** and **16**?

> **Open my eyes that I may see wonderful things in you law.**
> **Psalm 119:18**

> **Your word is a lamp to my feet and a light for my path.**
> **Psalm 119:105**

14) In **verse 8**, God says **I am the Lord, that is My name!** What does the name **Lord** mean to you?

15) How is God described in **verse 13**? Why is this characteristic of God important? Can you describe a time when God zealously prevailed in your life?

> **For a long time I have kept silent. I have been**
> **quiet and held myself back. But now, like a woman**
> **in childbirth, I cry out, I gasp and pant.**
> **Isaiah 42:14**

    This is an interesting view of God. He is very patient, but we humans certainly test His patience. He was anxious to send His Messiah Servant to triumph over the enemy and save us. And He is anxious to send Jesus a second time to gather us to Himself. Yet, He does not want anyone to perish. **For God so loved the world that he gave His one and only Son that whoever believes in Him shall not perish, but have eternal life (John 3:16).** God is patient, beyond our understanding!

16) Can you look back in your life and describe a time when God was particularly patient with you?

> **Set me free from my prison, that I may praise Your name.**
> **Psalm 142:7**
>
> **Blessed is he whose help is the God of Jacob, whose hope is in the Lord his God . . . The Lord sets prisoners free, the Lord gives sight to the blind, the Lord lifts up those who are bowed down.**
> **Psalm 146:5-8**

Before you go: Consider how the Lord specifically revealed Himself to you today. What words or phrases caught your attention? How do you respond to this? Lift a prayer of praise to the Lord.

Further Thoughts:

God tells us that His name is Lord (**Isaiah 42:8**). What do the following verses teach us about this name?

Exodus 20:2-3—

Mark 12:35-37—

Acts 2:34-36—

Philippians 2:9-11—

Our Savior and Redeemer

Lesson 13: Isaiah Chapters 43-46

This week's memory verse:

> **Fear not, for I have redeemed you; I have summoned you by name; you are mine.**
> **Isaiah 43:1**

Before you begin: Please start by praying to God. Give Him praise. Ask Him to reveal Himself and to speak to you today through this lesson.

Please read Isaiah Chapter 43.

God does not just sit on His heavenly throne and look down upon man. Our God is a God of action. He creates, redeems, calls, saves, and forgives. Hallelujah!

1) God is our Creator (**verses 1, 7, 15,** and **21**). According to **verses 7** and **21**, why did God create us, for what purpose?

2) God has redeemed us (**verse 1**). What does this mean? What has He redeemed us from? Use the following verses to answer the question: **Psalm 130:7-8**, **Galatians 4:4-5**, and **Ephesians 1:7-8**.

3) God has called or summoned us (**verses 1, 5-7**). Why does He call us? Look up the following verses to discover why He has called you. How do you feel being called or summoned by God?

John 6:44-45—

Acts 2:38-39—

Romans 8:28-30—

2 Timothy 1:9—

4) Where is God when you pass through the waters? What does He promise when you walk through the rivers and fire? What do the water and fire represent, according to **Psalm 66:10-12** and **Psalm 69:1-3, 13-15**?

> **He reached down from on high and took hold of me; He drew me out of deep waters.**
> **Psalm 18:16**

5) God is our Savior (**verses 3, 11-13**). Can you think of a time when He rescued you?

6) According to **verse 4**, why does our Creator God redeem and save us? What does **Ephesians 2:1-5** tell us?

> **Though you have made me see troubles, many and bitter, You will restore my life again; from the depths of the earth You will again bring me up. You will increase my honor and comfort me once again.**
> **Psalm 71:20-21**

"Because he loves me," says the Lord, "I will rescue him; I will protect him, for he acknowledges my name. He

> will call upon me, and I will answer him; I will be with him in trouble, I will deliver him and honor him."
> **Psalm 91:14-15**

> The Lord your God is with you, He is mighty to save. He will take great delight in you, He will quiet you with His love, He will rejoice over you with singing.
> **Zephaniah 3:17**

7) What distresses or upsets God in **verses 22-24**? What does He want us to do?

8) What does our loving and merciful God do for us in **verse 25**?

> But God demonstrates His own love for us in this: While we were still sinners, Christ died for us.
> **Romans 5:8**

> At that time, I will deal with all who oppressed you; I will rescue the lame and gather those who have been scattered. I will give them praise and honor in every land where they were put to shame. At that time, I will gather you; at that time, I will bring you home. I will give you honor and praise.
> **Zephaniah 3:19-20**

Please read Isaiah Chapter 44.

In this chapter, we see the foolishness of worshiping idols. We can feel the intensity. God is incensed! Today we do not make idols and worship them. . . or do we? Even as

Christians, we may have something so sacred, almost magical, that by touching it, we hope God will hear us, or keep us safe, (maybe the cross around our neck or a picture or something someone has brought us from the Holy Land). An idol is anything we value more than God, anything that we trust in instead of God, or that we run to before seeking God's help.

9) **Verses 1-2** and **24** remind us that God formed and made us; He chose us! What does it mean to be chosen by God? How do you feel about being chosen by God? What does **Ephesians 1:4-6, 11** and **I Peter 2:9** teach us about being chosen? How should we respond to this?

10) What will God give to us in **verse 3**? What do we learn about His Spirit in the following verses?

Luke 11:13—

John 14:26—

Romans 8:9-11—

11) When a woman marries, she often changes her last name to her husband's. And an adopted child accepts the name of his/her adoptive parents. What is God's desire in **verse 5**? What do we learn further from **Jeremiah 31:33-34** and **2 Corinthians 6:16**?

> **Him who overcomes... I will write on him the name of my God and the name of the city of my God, the new Jerusalem which is coming down out of heaven from my God; and I will write on him my new name.**
> **Revelation 3:12**

12) What has God done for us in **verse 22**? What does He want us to do? How does creation respond to this in **verse 23**?

> **Let the heavens rejoice, let the earth be glad; let the sea resound, and all that is in it; let the fields be jubilant, and everything in them. Then all the trees of the forest will sing for joy.**
> **Psalm 96:11-12**

God has not forgotten us! He will redeem us and remove our sins **like the morning mist**!

13) In **verses 6-7** God challenges the idols/gods to foretell what will happen. Then in **verses 24-28**, He predicts that his people will return and rebuild Jerusalem. Who has God named to make this happen?

Remember, Isaiah lived around 700 BC. At this time, the northern kingdom has been captured by the Assyrians, but Judah and Jerusalem have not. Two hundred years later, in 586 BC, Nebuchadnezzar captures Jerusalem. And in 538 BC, Cyrus, King of Persia, declares a temple to be built for the God of Heaven in Jerusalem. See **Ezra 1:1-2**. In 516 BC, the temple is completed, 70 years after it was destroyed. God told His people that Cyrus will rebuild the temple 200 years before it happened!

> **They finished building the temple according to the command of the God of Israel and the decrees of Cyrus, Darius, and Artaxerxes kings of Persia.**
> **Ezra 6:14**

> **I will praise You, O Lord with all my heart; before the**

> "gods" I will sing Your praise. I will bow down toward
> Your holy temple and I will praise Your name for
> Your love and Your faithfulness, for You have exalted
> above all things Your name and Your word.
> Psalm 138:1-2

Please read Isaiah Chapter 45.

> I am the Lord, and there is no other, apart
> from me there is no God.
> Isaiah 45:5

As you read the chapter, note the many phrases repeated: **So that you will know that I am the Lord. I am the Lord, there is no other god.** God is the Lord, the Holy One of Israel our Righteous God and Savior. He made the earth and all mankind for His purpose. Before Him, every knee will bow, and every tongue will confess that He is Lord.

14) God continues the prophecy that He will raise up Cyrus (**verses 1-6**). What were God's purposes according to **verses 6** and **13**?

> For by Him all things were created: things in
> heaven and on earth, visible and invisible, whether
> thrones or powers or rulers or authorities;
> all things were created by Him and for Him.
> Colossians 1:16

15) What is God's desire in **verses 22-24**? What does He want us to do?

Therefore, God exalted Him to the highest place and gave Him the name that is above every name, that at the name of Jesus

> every knee should bow, in heaven and on earth and under the
> earth, and every tongue confess that Jesus Christ is Lord,
> to the glory of God, the Father.
> **Philippians 2:9-11**

> **Come let us bow down and worship, let us
> kneel before the Lord our Maker.
> Psalm 95:6**

Please read **Isaiah Chapter 46**.

16) What has God been doing in **verse 3**? What does He promise in **verse 4**?

> **You yourselves have seen what I did to Egypt, and how I
> carried you on eagles' wings and brought you to myself.
> Exodus 19:4**

> **And in the desert, there you saw how the Lord your
> God carried you, as a father carries his son, all the
> way you went until you reached this place.
> Deuteronomy 1:31**

> **In a desert land He found him in a barren and howling
> waste. He shielded him and cared for him; He guarded
> him as the apple of His eye, like an eagle that stirs up
> its nest and hovers over its young, that spreads it wings
> to catch them and carries them on its pinions. The
> Lord alone led him; no foreign god was with him.
> Deuteronomy 32:10-12**

17) What does God ask us to do in **verse 9**? What do you remember from Bible stories or from your own life that remind you that there is no other god but our God?

> **For everything that was written in the past was**

> written to teach us, so that through endurance and the encouragement of the Scriptures we might have hope.
> Romans 15:4

18) What evidence have you found in God's Word, or in your own life, that God's **purpose will stand. . . What I have said, that will I bring about; what I have planned that will I do (verse 10-11)**?

19) What do we learn from **verse 13**?

> God made Him who had no sin to be sin for us, so that in Him we might become the righteousness of God.
> 2 Corinthians 5:21

> "In the time of my favor I heard you, and in the day of salvation I helped you." I tell you now is the time of God's favor, now is the day of salvation.
> 2 Corinthians 6:2

> Do not cast me away when I am old, do not forsake me when my strength is gone. . . Even when I am old and gray, do not forsake me, O God, till I declare Your power to the next generation, Your might to all who are to come. Your righteousness reaches to the skies, O God. You have done great things, who, O God is like You? . . . But as for me, I will always have hope. I will praise You more and more. My mouth will tell of Your righteousness, of Your salvation all day long, though I know not its measure.
> Psalm 71

Before you go: Consider how the Lord specifically revealed Himself to you today. What words or phrases caught your attention? How do you respond to this? Lift a prayer of praise to the Lord.

Further Thoughts:

1) Our God is a jealous God. He does not want us to share our affections with another. He wants our full devotion. Read **Ezekiel 16:1-42, 59-63**. Can you feel His passion? Please write your thoughts. If you are willing, write a prayer of devotion to God.

2) God raised up Cyrus for a purpose. Can you think of others who were raised for a purpose? Who were they and for what purpose? The following verses offer a few examples.

Exodus 9:16—

Jeremiah 1:4-5—

Luke 1:76-77—

Acts 2:22-24—

Ephesians 3:7-11—

Merciful God

Lesson 14: Isaiah Chapters 47-49

This week's memory verse:

> **His mercy extends to those who fear Him,
> from generation to generation.
> Luke 1:50**

Before you begin: Please start by praying to God. Give Him praise. Ask Him to reveal Himself and to speak to you today through this lesson.

Please read Isaiah Chapter 47.

This is a prophecy against Babylon. And in the midst of His anger toward Babylon, He reminds us that He is **Our Redeemer—the Lord Almighty is His name—is the Holy One of Israel. (verse 4).**

1) God gave His people into the hands of the Babylonians. Why was He so angry with the Babylonians? (**vs. 6**).

2) What are other reasons God opposed the Babylonians?

Verse 10—

Verse 12—

Verse 13—

3) The Babylonians did not trust in the True God. They trusted in themselves, in sorcery and astrology. According to **Leviticus 19:26** and **Deuteronomy 4:19; 8:10-20,** what does God say about this? What is the final outcome for those who practice this, according to **Revelation 21:8** and **22:15**?

4) **Psalm 74** was written while God's people were in Babylon. What was their response to God according **to Psalm 74:1-2, 18-23?**

> **You showed favor to Your land, O Lord; You restored the fortunes of Jacob. You forgave the iniquity of Your people and covered all their sins. You set aside all Your wrath and turned from Your fierce anger. Restore us again, O God our Savior and put away Your displeasure toward us... Show us Your unfailing love, O Lord, and grant us Your salvation.**
> **Psalm 85:1-4, 7**

> **My soul glorifies the Lord, and my spirit rejoices in God my Savior... He has performed mighty deeds with His arm; He has scattered those who are proud in their inmost thoughts. He has brought down rulers from their thrones but has lifted up the humble. He has filled the hungry with good things but has sent the rich away empty. He has helped His servant Israel, remembering to be merciful to Abraham and His descendants forever, even as he said to our fathers.**
> **Luke 1:46-47, 51-55**

Please read Isaiah Chapter 48.

God's people claim the name of the God of Israel, call to Him and make oaths to Him, yet their cries are empty. They have no faith in Him, so they turn to their idols. God tells them, **Therefore I told you these things long ago; before they happened, I announced them to you so that you could not say, "My idols did them; my wooden image and metal god ordained them." (verse 5)**. Remember that these prophecies were given about 200 years before they happened.

As Christians, we too cry out to our God, yet our words are empty. We really do not expect God to answer our prayers, and we are surprised when He does. Or maybe we really do not believe that Jesus is returning. After all, people have been predicting it for 2000 years.

5) Look up the following verses and record what Jesus told His disciples.

Matthew 12:40—

Matthew 16:21—

Matthew 20:18-19—

John 10:11, 17—

John 14:28-29—

Jesus told His disciples many times what would happen, yet they were shocked and grieved when Jesus was taken and crucified. And they were surprised and in disbelief when He rose from the dead! Do not be so hard on the disciples, for God has given us many promises and we, too, when in distress and despair, are taken by surprise when He honors them.

6) Describe a time when God refined you or tested you in the **furnace of affliction (verse 10)**.

> **Examine me, O Lord and prove me; Try my mind and my heart.**
> **Psalm 26:2**

> **Blessed is the man who perseveres under trial, because when he has stood the test, he will receive the crown of life that God has promised to those who love Him.**
> **James 1:12**

7) How does God teach and direct us? Describe a time when He taught you something or directed you **(verse 17)**. What does **Psalm 119:33-37** tells us?

8) What is the reward for those who listen and follow His teaching and direction **(verse 18)**?

> **Great peace have they who love your law.**
> **Psalm 119:165**

> **The mind controlled by the Spirit is life and peace.**
> **Romans 8:6**

9) According to **verses 9** and **11**, why does God do all of this?

> **But He said to me, "My grace is sufficient for you, for my power is made perfect in weakness." Therefore, I will boast all the more gladly about my weaknesses, so that Christ's power may rest on me. That is why, for Christ's sake, I delight**

> in weaknesses, in insults, in hardships, in persecutions, in difficulties. For when I am weak, then I am strong.
> 2 Corinthians 12:9-10

> And whatever you do, whether in word or deed, do it all in the name of the Lord Jesus, giving thanks to God the Father through Him.
> Colossians 3:17

> Behold, I am coming soon! My reward is with me, and I will give to everyone according to what he has done.
> Revelation 22:12

Please read Isaiah Chapter 49.

> Can a mother forget the baby at her breast and have no compassion on the child she has borne? Though she may forget, I will not forget you!
> Isaiah 49:15

God has not forgotten His people. He hears their cry and is now ready to take action. Our God is a God of action. While he calls His people back from Babylon, He also tells us He plans to gather all of us from the ends of the world to Him. Jesus is coming back to take us home!

10) The second Servant Messiah prophecy is found in the first seven verses of this chapter. Look at each verse and compare with the corresponding scriptures to see how Jesus fulfills this prophecy.

Verse 1: Luke 1:31-33—

Verse 2: Revelation 1:13-18—

Verse 3: John 1:14—

Verses 4-5, 7: Philippians 2:6-11—

Verse 6: Luke 24:46-47—

> **All the ends of the earth will remember and turn to the Lord, and all the families of the nations will bow down before Him, for dominion belongs to the Lord and He rules over the nations... They will proclaim His righteousness to a people yet unborn—for He has done it.**
> **Psalm 22:27-28, 31**

11) Read verses **8-16** again and look for action words. What does God promise He will do for His people? How has God acted in this way in your life?

God answers, helps, restores, sets free, satisfies the hungry and thirsty, has compassion on us, guides, comforts, and remembers us! It seems absurd to us that a mother would forget her child, yet it does happen. **Though she may forget, I will not forget you!** And did you notice—God has a tattoo! He has engraved your name on the palm of His hands!

12) Why does God do all of this according to verses **23** and **26**?

> **But I, when I am lifted up from the earth, will draw all men to myself.**
> **John 12:32**

At that time men will see the Son of Man coming in clouds with great power and glory. And He will send His angels and gather His elect from the four winds, from the ends of the earth to the ends of the heavens.
Mark 13:26-27

In my Father's house are many rooms. If it were not so, I would have told you. I ˋam going there to prepare a place for you. And if I go and prepare a place for you, I will come back and take you to be with me that you also may be where I am.
John 14:2-3

Before you go: Consider how the Lord specifically revealed Himself to you today. What words or phrases caught your attention? How do you respond to this? Lift a prayer of praise to the Lord.

Further Thoughts:

1) The Servant Messiah says in **Isaiah 49:2, He made my mouth like a sharpened sword.** What does the sharpened sword symbolize? **John 1:1-2, 14** tells us that Jesus is the Word of God. As we consider these, read the following verses and write your thoughts:

    Ephesians 6:17—

    Hebrews 4:12—

    Revelation 2:12, 16—

Revelation 19:13, 15 and **21**—

2) The Servant Messiah says in **Isaiah 49:4, And my reward is with My God**. What do you think is His reward? See also **Isaiah 40:10; 62:11-12**. Consider **John 17:2, Revelation 5:12,** and **Revelation 19:6-9**. What could be other ideas?

Sovereign Teacher

Lesson 15: Isaiah Chapters 50 - 52:1-12

This week's memory verse:

> **But you, dear friends, build yourselves up in your most holy faith and pray in the Holy Spirit. Keep yourselves in God's love as you wait for the mercy of our Lord Jesus Christ to bring you to eternal life.**
> **Jude 20-21**

Before you begin: Please start by praying to God. Give Him praise. Ask Him to reveal Himself and to speak to you today through this lesson.

Please read Isaiah Chapter 50.

It was because of their iniquities that God sent away His people; because of their transgressions He sold them. But He knew it was not permanent. He did not give them a certificate of divorce because He already planned to save them. **Was my arm too short to ransom you? Do I lack the strength to rescue you? (Isaiah 50:2)** In this chapter, we find the third Servant Messiah prophecies. God bears His heart to us. He longs for a relationship with His people.

> **When I came, why was there no one? When I called, why was there no one to answer?**
> **Isaiah 50:2**

1) What did God do in **verse 2**? How did His people respond? As you read what God said, what emotions do you think God expressed in **verses 1-3**?

> **I am the Lord, the God of all mankind. Is
> anything too hard for me?**
> **Jeremiah 32:27**

2) According to **Mark 1:35** and **15:1-5,15-20**, how does Jesus fulfill the prophecy of the Servant Messiah in **verses 4-9**?

3) Describe a time when God gave you His wisdom and instruction or gave you the words to say at the right time (**verse 4**).

> **I will instruct you and teach you in the way you should go;
> I will counsel you and watch over you.**
> **Psalm 32:8**

4) In **verses 8-9**, God tells us he will contend for us, He will vindicate and help us. Describe a time when God defended you, acted on your behalf. (See also **Isaiah 49:25**). What do we learn from **Psalm 27:1-3** and **Romans 8:31-34**?

5) Understanding that Jesus is the Servant described in **verse 10**, what are some of the commands that Jesus gave us to obey? Use scripture to support your answer.

6) In **verse 10**, God desires those who walk in darkness to trust

and rely on Him. According to **verse 11**, what will happen to them if they do not put their trust in Him? What did Jesus say in **Matthew 13:49-50**?

> **Praise the Lord. Blessed is the man who fears the Lord, who finds delight in His commands. . . Wealth and riches are in his house and his righteousness endures forever. Even in darkness light dawns for the upright, for the gracious and compassionate and righteous man. . . Surely, he will never be shaken; a righteous man will be remembered forever. He will have no fear of bad news; his heart is steadfast, trusting the Lord. His heart is secure, he will have no fear; in the end he will look in triumph on his foes. . . The wicked man will see and be vexed, he will gnash his teeth and waste away; the longings of the wicked will come to nothing.**
> **Psalm 112**

> **Ah, Sovereign Lord, You have made the heavens and the earth by Your great power and outstretched arm. Nothing is too hard for you.**
> **Jeremiah 32:17**

Please read Isaiah 51-52:12.

Listen! Listen! Awake, awake! God wants to capture our attention! God assures His people that He will bring them back to Jerusalem, to Zion. But as we look closer at these chapters, God is not describing the return of his people from Babylon, but the end of days when all of us, His people, will enter into our heavenly home!

7) What does God tell us in **Isaiah 51:6-8**? What do we learn from **Hebrews 1:10-12**? What assurance does God give us in this verse?

> **He became the source of eternal salvation**
> **for all who obey Him.**
> **Hebrews 5:9**

8) What assurance does God give us in **Isaiah 51:7-8** and **12**?

9) What does God promise in verse 11? Describe how His people respond.

> **The ransomed of the Lord will return. They**
> **will enter Zion with singing;**
> **everlasting joy will crown their heads. Gladness**
> **and joy will overtake them,**
> **and sorrow and sighing will flee away.**
> **Isaiah 51:11**

10) As God's people enter into Zion, what garments are they wearing according to **Isaiah 52:1**? What do these garments represent? See **Revelation 3:5** and **7:9, 13-14**.

> **I saw the Holy City, the new Jerusalem coming**
> **down out of heaven from God,**
> **prepared as a bride beautifully dressed for her husband.**
> **Revelation 21:2**

> **O Zion . . . the uncircumcised and undefiled**
> **will not enter you again.**
> **Isaiah 52:1**

> **Blessed are the pure in heart, for they will see God.**

Matthew 5:8

All glorious is the princess within her chamber; her gown is interwoven with gold. In embroidered garments she is led to the King; her virgin companions follow her and are brought to you. They are led in with joy and gladness; they enter the palace of the King.
Psalm 45:13-15

11) What pleases God in **Isaiah 52:7**? Give an example of how you can do this.

I proclaim righteousness in the great assembly; I do not seal my lips, as you know, O Lord. I do not hide Your righteousness in my heart; I speak of Your faithfulness and salvation. I do not conceal Your love and Your truth from the great assembly.
Psalm 40:9-10

Blessed are the peacemakers, for they
will be called sons of God.
Matthew 5:9

12) What has God done for His people in **Isaiah 52:9-10**? What does He promise?

Sing to the Lord a new song, for He has done marvelous things;
His right hand and His holy arm have
worked salvation for Him.
The Lord has made His salvation known and
revealed His righteousness to the nations.
He has remembered His love and His
faithfulness to the house of Israel;
all the ends of the earth have seen the salvation of our God.
Psalm 98:1-3

13) What does God promise us in **Isaiah 52:12**?

   a) Give an example describing when God went before you, maybe prepared you or circumstances around you ahead of time.

   b) Give an example describing when God was your rear guard, maybe helped you or protected you after an event.

> **The Lord Himself goes before you and will be with you; He will never leave you nor forsake you. Do not be afraid; do not be discouraged.**
> **Deuteronomy 31:8**

Before you go: Consider how the Lord specifically revealed Himself to you today. What words or phrases caught your attention? How do you respond to this? Lift a prayer of praise to the Lord.

Further Thoughts:

1) In **Isaiah 51:1**, God asks us to **look to the rock from which you were cut**. Who is the Rock according to **Isaiah 26:4**? What do we learn about our relationship with God in **Genesis 1:27** and **Colossians 3:1-10**?

2) God asks us to look to the Rock; look to Abraham and Sarah (**Isaiah 51:1-2**). What can we learn by looking back to the beginnings of our faith? Read **Hebrews 11:8-19** for insight.

Lover of My Soul

Lesson 16: Isaiah Chapter 52:13-15 and Chapters 53-55

This week's memory verse:

> **Greater love has no one than this, that He lay down His life for His friends.**
> **John 15:13**

Before you begin: Please start by praying to God. Give Him praise. Ask Him to reveal Himself and to speak to you today through this lesson.

Please read Isaiah Chapters 52:13-15 and 53.

Oh, the depth of God's love! In these verses God shows us His intense, passionate love for us. He will stop at nothing to save us and bring us to Himself, including sacrificing His own Son, Jesus Christ for us.

> **For God so loved the world that He gave His one and only Son, that whoever believes in Him shall not perish but have eternal life.**
> **John 3:16**

This is the fourth and final Servant Messiah prophecy. Christ Jesus, **Who, being in very nature God, did not consider equality with God something to be grasped, but made himself nothing, taking the very nature of a servant, being made in human likeness. And being found in appearance as a man, He humbled himself and became obedient to death—even death on a cross. Philippians 2:6-8.**

1) In what specific ways did Jesus fulfill this prophecy? You may want to review the last few chapters of **Matthew, Mark, Luke, and John.**

> **When evening had come, they brought to Him many who were demon possessed. And He cast out the spirits with a word, and healed all who were sick, that it might be fulfill which was spoken by Isaiah the prophet, saying: "He Himself took our infirmities and bore our sicknesses."**
> **Matthew 8:16-17**

2) How is Jesus described in the following verses? **John 1:29, I Peter 1:18-19**, and **Revelation 5:6-14**.

3) What was God's will in **verse 10**? What is a guilt or sin offering according to **Leviticus 5:17-19**? How did Jesus feel in **Mark 14:32-36** the night before He was crucified?

> **God made Him who had no sin to be sin for us, so that in Him we might become the righteousness of God.**
> **2 Corinthians 5:21**

> **He is the atoning sacrifice for our sins, and not only for ours but also for the sins of the whole world.**
> **I John 2:2**

4) What is the true heart of God in these verses? Why was Jesus sacrificed? For whom? What do these verses tell us about the heart of God? **I John 4:9-10, Romans 5:8**, and **Romans 8:32**?

God loves you so much that He gave His one and only Son

to be sacrificed for your sins. Let me say that again! God loves you so much that He gave His one and only Son to be sacrificed for your sins!

5) How can we even begin to respond to such love? Consider the following verses: **Romans 12:1-2**, and **Romans 13:8** and **I John 4:11**. How else can we respond to God's love? Can you find verses to support your answer?

6) Worship God by reading **Psalm 103**.

> **Show me the wonder of your great love...**
> **Keep me as the apple of your eye.**
> **Psalm 17:7-8**

> **Because of the Lord's great love, we are not consumed, for His compassions never fail. Lamentations 3:22**

> **For even the Son of Man did not come**
> **to be served, but to serve,**
> **and to give His life as a ransom for many.**
> **Mark 10:45**

Please read Isaiah Chapter 54.

Our God just demonstrated unimaginable, sacrificial love, giving Himself up for us. He now takes us deeper to a relationship so intimate that He can only be described as our Husband. Like an earthly husband, God's love is unconditional and unfailing. He provides for us, protects us, instructs us, and leads us. He desires our undivided devotion and faithfulness.

> **For your Maker is your husband—the Lord Almighty**
> **is His name—the Holy One of Israel is your**
> **Redeemer, He is called the God of all the earth.**

Isaiah 54:5

7) List the qualities or roles of a husband. How would you describe the relationship between a husband and a wife? How does God describe Himself in **Hosea 2:16** and **19-20**?

8) In Biblical days, the symbolism of spreading the corner of your garment over someone was to enter into a contract of marriage. What a beautiful, intimate image, an image of protection, oneness, and vulnerability. What does Ruth ask Boaz in **Ruth 3:9**? And what was the result of her boldness in **Ruth 4:13-14**?

> **Later I passed by, and when I looked at you and saw that you were old enough for love, I spread the corner of my garment over you and covered your nakedness. I gave you my solemn oath and entered into a covenant with you, declares the Sovereign Lord, and you became mine.**
> **Ezekiel 16:8**

> **He anointed us, set His seal of ownership on us, and put His Spirit in our hearts as a deposit, guaranteeing what is to come.**
> **2 Corinthians 1:21-22**

9) God entered into a Covenant Relationship with His people and then they left Him and turned to other gods. God desires faithfulness to Him! What emotions does God show in **verses 6-8**? How does He respond to His people? How do these emotions compare to those God revealed in **Hosea 2:13-14** and **Hosea 11:8-9**?

> **Be careful not to forget the covenant of the Lord your God that He made with you, do not make for yourselves an idol in the form of anything the Lord your God has forbidden. For the Lord your God is a consuming fire, a jealous God.**
> **Deuteronomy 4:23-24**

10) God loves us. How does God describe this love in **verses 4-8**? What does God promise us in **verse 10**?

> **You have stolen My heart, My sister, My bride; you have stolen My heart with one glance of your eyes, with one jewel of your necklace. How delightful is your love, My sister, My bride! How much more pleasing is your love than wine, and the fragrance of your perfume than any spice!**
> **Song of Songs 4:9-10**

11) God provides for us. In Biblical days, the bridegroom left to build a home for his bride. In **verses 11-12** God tells us that He is going to build a city with precious stones. We see in Nehemiah that Jerusalem was not rebuilt with precious stones. Instead, God is describing our future home! How does this compare with **Revelation 21:9-27**?

> **In my Father's house are many rooms... I am going there to prepare a place for you... I will come back and take you to be with Me that you also may be where I am.**
> **John 14:2-3**

12) God teaches us. What does He promise in **verse 13**?

13) God is our Protector. What does He promise in **verses 14-17?** What is our heritage from the Lord in **verse 17?**

It may seem odd to think of God as our Husband, but when we think of who God is and our relationship with Him, it makes sense. He has entered into a covenant relationship with us through the blood of Jesus Christ. He gives us the honor of His Name. God loves us more extravagantly than any human can. He desires our faithfulness and becomes jealous when we turn away from Him. He provides for us and protects us. He is preparing a special home for us, His bride, where we will be able to spend eternity with Him.

> **And I pray that you being rooted and established in love, may have power together will all the saints, to grasp how wide and long and high and deep is the love of Christ and to know this love that surpasses knowledge—that you may be filled to the measure of all the fullness of God.**
> **Ephesians 3:17-19**

> **I will sing of the Lord's great love forever; with my mouth I will make Your faithfulness known through all generations. I will declare that Your love stands firm forever and that You established Your faithfulness in heaven itself.**
> **Psalm 89:1-2**

Please read Isaiah Chapter 55.

God loves us beyond understanding. He calls Himself our Husband, the name of the most intimate of human relationships. He now calls us to Him, to enter into sweet communion with Him and become one with Him.

As you read this chapter, oh, can you feel God's heart? **Come. . . come. . . come. . . listen, listen to me. . . give ear and come to me. . . Seek the Lord. . . call on Him.**

14) Read **Luke 10:38-41**. What does Jesus want us to do?

> **My Lover spoke and said to me, "Arise my darling,**
> **my beautiful one and come with me."**
> **Song of Songs 2:10**

> **I delight to sit in His shade and His fruit is sweet**
> **to my taste. He has taken me to the banquet**
> **hall and His banner over me is love.**
> **Song of Songs 2:3-4**

And the Lover of our soul replies:

> **Show me your face, let me hear your voice, for**
> **your voice is sweet and your face is lovely.**
> **Song of Songs 2:14**

15) **Come, all who are thirsty (verse 1).** What did Jesus proclaim in **John 7:37-38**?

> **He said to me, "It is done. I am the Alpha and the Omega, the**
> **Beginning and the End. To him who is thirsty I will give to**
> **drink without cost from the spring of the water of life."**
> **Revelation 21:6**

> **Whoever is thirsty, let him come and**
> **whoever wishes let him take the**
> **free gift of the water of life.**

Revelation 22:17

16) **Come, buy and eat! . . . and your soul will delight in the richest of fare (verses 1-2).** What does God mean by these words? What did Jesus proclaim in **John 6:35, 51, and 53-58**?

> **And He took bread, gave thanks and broke it, and gave it to them, saying, "This is my body given for you: do this in remembrance of me." In the same way, after supper He took the cup, saying, "This cup is the new covenant in my blood, which is poured out for you."**
> **Luke 22:19-20**

> **Taste and see that the Lord is good.**
> **Psalm 34:8**

> **Blessed are those who hunger and thirst for righteousness, for they will be filled.**
> **Matthew 5:6**

Whenever we take Communion, we remember what Jesus has done for us. We eat the bread that reminds us of His body given for us. We drink the juice as a reminder of the blood He shed for us. We become one with Him.

17) What does God promise us in **verse 3**? What does God tell us in **Jeremiah 31:3** and
50:4-5?

> **"I spread the corner of my garment over you. . . I gave you my solemn oath and entered into a covenant with you," declares the Lord, "and you became Mine."**
> **Ezekiel 16:8**

> **From everlasting to everlasting the Lord's
> love is with those who fear Him.
> Psalm 103:17**

18) What does God desire in **verse 6**?

19) What does God desire of the wicked in **verse 7**? How does He respond to them? How did Jesus respond to the criminal in **Luke 23:39-43**?

> **He himself bore our sins in His body on the tree, so
> that we might die to sins and live for righteousness;
> by His wounds you have been healed. For you were
> like sheep going astray, but now you have returned
> to the Shepherd and Overseer of your souls.
> I Peter 2:24-25**

20) What assurance do we find in **verses 10-11**?

> **The Lord is faithful to all His promises and
> loving toward all He has made.
> Psalm 145:13**

> **If anyone acknowledges that Jesus is the Son of
> God, God lives in him and he in God.
> ... God is love. Whoever lives in love,
> lives in God, and God in him.
> I John 4:15-16**

> **But he who unites himself with the Lord
> is one with Him in spirit.
> I Corinthians 6:17**

We have reached the pinnacle, the climax of the Book of Isaiah. God's love for us is overwhelming. He desires a deep, rich, close, loving relationship with Him. And He will do anything to captivate us and bring us to Him. He wants to be God With Us! He wants to be our God and us His people. Let us love the Lord not because He saved us or blesses us or promises us heaven. Let us love Him because of who He is. We do not love our husbands or children, friends, or others because of what they can do for us. We just love them. So it is with God. Let us love Him, truly love Him, and bask in His love for us.

O God, You are my God, earnestly I seek You; my soul thirsts for You in a dry and weary land where there is no water... Because Your love is better than life, my lips will glorify you... My soul will be satisfied as with the riches of foods.
Psalm 63:1 ,3, 5

Before you go: Consider how the Lord specifically revealed Himself to you today. What words or phrases caught your attention? How do you respond to this? Lift a prayer of praise to the Lord.

Further Thoughts: You may wish to participate in a Communion Service with this lesson. Please consider the Communion Devotion in the Appendix.

Loving Others

Lesson 17: Isaiah Chapters 56-59

This week's memory verse:

> **Dear friends, since God so loved us, we also ought to love one another.**
> **I John 4:11**

Before you begin: Please start by praying to God. Give Him praise. Ask Him to reveal Himself and to speak to you today through this lesson.

Please read Isaiah Chapter 56.

God loves us so much and desires us to share His love with others. Sin hinders that love. We harbor prejudice and hatred, and an "us-against-them" attitude. In this chapter, two groups of people were considered as having less value: the eunuchs who were not able to produce heirs and the foreigners or Gentiles. However, there is no distinction in God's eyes. He loves all the people He has created and wants us to love them as well.

1) What do **verses 1-2** tell us about God's salvation? What does God want us to do?

2) If you are not Jewish, then you are a Gentile or foreigner. This chapter speaks for the majority of us. Not all foreigners will be able to enter God's Holy Mountain (heaven). According to **verses 3** and **6**, what distinguishes these foreigners from others?

3) Please read **Matthew 22:1-14 and 25:1-13**. What do we learn from these parables? What is the difference between those who enter the wedding feast and those who do not? How can we be prepared? Read **Philippians 3:7-14** for insight.

4) What does it mean to bind or join ourselves to the Lord? What do we learn about the servant in **Exodus 21:5-6** and in **Philippians 3:7-14**?

> **Remember, O Lord, how I have walked before you faithfully and with wholehearted devotion and have done what is good in your eyes.**
> **Isaiah 38:3**

5) Who are the others God will gather in **verse 8** and in **John 10:16**?

> **God our Savior, who wants all men to be saved and to come to a knowledge of the truth. For there is one God and one mediator between God and men, the man Christ Jesus who gave himself as a ransom for all men.**
> **I Timothy 2:3-6**

6) What prejudices or hindrances are keeping you from loving others as God does?

> **The second is this: Love your neighbor as yourself.**
> **Mark 12:31**

> **You have heard that it was said, Love your neighbor
> and hate your enemy. But I tell you, love your
> enemies and pray for those who persecute you.**
> **Matthew 5:43-44**

> **Sing to the Lord a new song; sing to the Lord, all the earth.
> Sing to the Lord, praise His name; proclaim His salvation
> day after day. Declare His glory among all peoples. For
> great is the Lord and most worthy of praise. . . Ascribe to the
> Lord, O families of nations. Ascribe to the Lord glory and
> strength. Ascribe to the Lord the glory due His name; bring
> an offering and come into His courts. Worship the Lord in the
> splendor of His holiness; tremble before Him all the earth.**
> **Psalm 96:1-9**

Because God loves us so much, He wants us to share His love with others. In **Isaiah Chapter 56** we addressed our prejudices and attitudes toward others. In **Isaiah Chapter 57**, we are challenged to forgive others, just as God has forgiven us.

> **Bear with each other and forgive whatever
> grievances you may have against one another.
> Forgive as the Lord forgave you.**
> **Colossians 3:13**

Please read Isaiah Chapter 57.

7) God is angry! Can you feel the intensity of His frustration and anger (**verses 6**, **13**, and **17**)? List the reasons for His anger as described in this chapter.

8) How does God describe Himself in **verses 15-16**? With whom does God dwell?

9) How does God respond to those who repent of their sins and humble themselves before Him (**vss. 16-19**)?

> **The Lord is compassionate and gracious,**
> **slow to anger, abounding in love.**
> **He will not always accuse, nor will He**
> **harbor His anger forever.**
> **He does not treat us as our sins deserve or**
> **repay us according to our iniquities.**
> **For as high as the heavens are above the earth, so**
> **great is His love for those who fear Him.**
> **As far as the east is from the west, so far has he**
> **removed our transgressions from us.**
> **Psalm 103:8-12**

10) If God can forgive extravagantly, so must we. Who do you need to forgive today? What do the following verses tell us about forgiveness?

Matthew 6:12, 14-15—

Matthew 18:21-22—

I John 4:19-21—

Please read Isaiah Chapter 58.
    We have learned to love indiscriminately and to forgive again and again. God wants us to now deepen our compassion for the oppressed. God's people seemed to be doing the right things. They fasted and prayed and honored the Sabbath, yet they did not have the right attitude. They were self-seeking. God's heart is for the poor, the widows, the fatherless, and the

afflicted. He wants us to love and care for them as He does.

11) Why was God displeased with His people (**verses 1-5**)? What did Jesus teach about prayer, fasting, and giving to others in **Matthew 6:1-18** and **7:21-23**?

12) What does God want us to do for those who are in need?

    a) What did Jesus teach in **Matthew 25:34-40**?

    b) What specific things can we do according to **Romans 12:9-18**?

13) According to this chapter, what does God promise those who help the afflicted and oppressed?

> **A generous man will prosper; he who refreshes others will himself be refreshed.**
> **Proverbs 11:25**
>
> **Give, and it will be given to you. A good measure, pressed down, shaken together and running over, will be poured into your lap. For with the measure you use, it will be measured to you.**
> **Luke 6:38**

14) How can you specifically show God's love to someone today?

Please read Isaiah Chapter 59.

    Once again, God reminds us of how sinful we are. Our iniquities have separated us from God and our sins have hidden

God's face from us. But there is hope.

> **Surely the arm of the Lord is not too short to**
> **save, nor His ear too dull to hear.**
> **Isaiah 59:1**

15) How is God described in **verse 1**? According to **verse 2**, why did God not hear the people's prayers?

16) Notice the differences in pronouns from **verses 2-3**, **4-8**, and **9-13**. Re-read **verses 1-15** using the pronouns "I", "me", and "my". For example: **But <u>my</u> iniquities have separated <u>me</u> from <u>my</u> God; <u>my</u> sins have hidden His face from <u>me</u>, so that He will not hear (verse 2).**

> **The Lord looked and was displeased that there was no justice.**
> **He saw that there was no one,**
> **He was appalled that there was no one to intervene.**
> **So, His own arm worked salvation for Him, and**
> **His own righteousness sustained Him.**
> **Isaiah 59:15-16**

17) **Verse 16** tells us God was appalled that there was no one to intervene, no one to save His people! So what did He do?

> **Surely, He took up our infirmities and carried our sorrows...**
> **He was pierced for our transgressions; He was crushed for**
> **our iniquities; the punishment that brought us peace was**
> **upon Him and by His wounds we are healed... He bore the**
> **sin of many and made intercession for the transgressors.**
> **Isaiah 53**
>
> **He was delivered over to death for our sins and**
> **was raised to life for our justification.**

Romans 4:25

18) According to **verse 17**, how did our Lord and Redeemer prepare to defeat our enemies? How does this compare with **Ephesians 6:10-18**? What can we learn from this?

19) Jesus Christ our Savior and Redeemer has not only saved us, but He promises to return to defeat our enemies and to take us home with Him (**verses 17-20**)! How does **Matthew 24:27-31** and **Revelation 19:11-21** describe this event? What are your thoughts regarding this event? Write a prayer of praise and thanksgiving.

> **Repent, then and turn to God, so that
> your sins may be wiped out,
> that times of refreshing my come from the Lord.
> Acts 3:19**
>
> **Search me, O God, and know my heart, test me and
> know my anxious thoughts. See if there is any offensive
> way in me, and lead me in the way everlasting.
> Psalm 139:23-24**
>
> **If you, O Lord, kept a record of sins, O Lord, who can stand?
> But with You there is forgiveness; therefore, You are
> feared. . . O Israel, put your hope in the Lord, for with the
> Lord is unfailing love and with Him is full redemption.
> He himself will redeem Israel from all their sins.
> Psalm 130:3-4,7-8**
>
> **You forgave the iniquity of Your people
> and covered all their sins. . .
> Restore us again, O God our Savior, and put
> away Your displeasure toward us. . .**

> **Show us Your unfailing love, O Lord, and
> grant us Your salvation.**
> **Psalm 85**

Before you go: Consider how the Lord specifically revealed Himself to you today. What words or phrases caught your attention? How do you respond to this? Lift a prayer of praise to the Lord.

Further Thoughts:

1) In our world today, so many fear death; we grieve for those who have gone before us. What comfort do we find in **Isaiah 57:1-2**? How is this different for the wicked in **Isaiah 57:20-21**? What do we learn from the following verses?

Psalm 23:4—

Psalm 116:15—

John 5:24—

I Corinthians 15:26, 50-57—

Hebrews 2:14-15—

Revelation 21:4—

2) What does God promise in **Isaiah 59: 21**? What did Jesus promise in **John 14:16-17** and **John 16:7-15**? What is the role of the Holy Spirit in our lives?

> **We know that we live in Him and He in us,**
> **because He has given us of His Spirit.**
> **I John 4:13**

> **Having believed, you were marked in Him with a seal,**
> **the promised Holy Spirit, who is a deposit guaranteeing**
> **our inheritance, until the redemption of those who**
> **are God's possession—to the praise of His glory.**
> **Ephesians 1:13-14**

God's Dwelling Place

Lesson 18: Isaiah Chapters 60-62

This week's memory verse:

> **I delight greatly in the Lord; my soul rejoices in my God; for He has clothed me with the garments of salvation and arrayed me in a robe of righteousness.**
> **Isaiah 61:10**

Before you begin: Please start by praying to God. Give Him praise. Ask Him to reveal Himself and to speak to you today through this lesson.

Have you wondered what our eternal home will be like, the new heavens and the new earth, where heaven and earth become one and God and mankind dwell together forever?

Randy Alcorn in his book *Heaven* writes, "The marriage of the God of Heaven with the people of earth will also bring the marriage of heaven and earth. There will not be two universes —one primary home of God and angels, the other the primary home of humanity. . . Nothing will separate us from God, and nothing will separate earth and heaven. Once God and mankind dwell together, there will be no difference between heaven and earth. Earth will become heaven and it will truly be heaven on earth. The new earth will be God's dwelling place."

And He made known to us the mystery of His will according to His good pleasure, which He purposed in Christ, to put into effect when the times will have reached their fulfillment— to bring all things in heaven and on earth together under

> **one head, even Christ.**
> **Ephesians 1:9-10**

Please read Isaiah Chapter 60.

1) What is the name of the city God is describing in **verse 14**? How is this city described in **Jeremiah 3:17; 33:16**, and **Ezekiel 48:35**?

2) ... **and I will glorify the place of my feet (verse 13).** Where do these verses tell us are God's feet? **Isaiah 66:1** and **Matthew 5:34-35**?

3) What do **verses 1-2** and **19-20** tell us about God? How does this compare with **Revelation 21:22-27**?

4) What does God promise in **verses 3-5** and **21**? For what purpose?

> **God, the Blessed, and only Ruler, the King of Kings and Lord of Lords, who alone is immortal and who lives in unapproachable light, whom no one has seen or can see, to Him be honor and might forever. Amen.**
> **I Timothy 6:15-16**

5) How should we respond to this hope of our eternal home with God? See **Hebrews 11:13-16; 12:22-29**.

> **Then you will know that I, the Lord your God, dwell in**

> Zion, my holy hill. Jerusalem will be holy; never again
> will foreigners invade her. In that day the mountains
> will drip new wine, and the hills will flow with milk;
> all the ravines of Judah will run with water.
> A fountain will flow out of the Lord's house
> and water the valley of acacias...
> Judah will be inhabited forever and Jerusalem
> through all generations.
> Their bloodguilt which I have not pardoned, I will pardon.
> The Lord dwells in Zion!
> Joel 3:17-21

Please read Isaiah Chapter 61.

6) **Read Luke 4:16-21.** What did Jesus say about this prophecy?

7) In **verses 1-3,** for whom does God's heart break, for whom does He have compassion? What does He want to do for them? For us?

> The Lord is close to the brokenhearted and
> saves those who are crushed in spirit.
> Psalm 34:18

> The sacrifices of God are a broken spirit;
> a broken and contrite heart,
> O God, you will not despise.
> Psalm 51:17

All of us at some time in our lives have been poor in spirit, brokenhearted, held captive by sin and darkness, and in need of comfort. Maybe you are experiencing this now. Allow Him to heal and comfort you. Praise Him for giving us joy and hope, a crown of beauty, the oil of joy and gladness, and a garment of praise.

8) According to the last part of **verse 3**, what will we be called? For what purpose? Why is righteousness important to God? What do the following verses teach us about righteousness? **2 Timothy 4:8, I Peter 2:24**, and **2 Peter 3:13**.

> **You heavens above, rain down righteousness;**
> **let the clouds shower it down.**
> **Let the earth open wide, let salvation spring**
> **up, let righteousness grow with it;**
> **I, the Lord, have created it.**
> **Isaiah 45:8**

9) In **verse 6** we are called priests of the Lord, servants or ministers of God. What is the role of a priest or a minister? How does this apply to us? Consider **I Peter 2:5, 9** and **Revelation 5:10**.

10) How does God give reward to His people according to **verse 7**? Can you give examples of this in scripture or in your own life?

11) What does God give us in **verse 10**? What does **2 Corinthians 5:1-5** tell us about His gift to us?

> **The righteous will flourish like a palm tree, they will**
> **grow like a cedar of Lebanon; planted in the house of**
> **the Lord, they will flourish in the courts of our God.**
> **Psalm 92:12-13**

12) As we reflect on this chapter, we see that God values righteousness. We can never be fully righteous without Jesus Christ our Savior. But that does not give us the excuse to sin and live ungodly lives. How do **Ephesians 5:15** and **Hebrews 10:23-25** tell us to live?

> **He carried me away in the Spirit to a mountain great and high, and showed me the Holy City, Jerusalem, coming down out of heaven from God. It shown with the glory of God, and its brilliance was like that of a very precious jewel, like jasper, clear as crystal.**
> **Revelation 21:10-11**

Please read Isaiah Chapter 62.

God is passionate about Zion, the new Jerusalem. He will not be silent until her righteousness and salvation shines. The current Jerusalem will never experience complete righteousness and salvation. God is describing our eternal home, the new heavenly Jerusalem.

13) How is the new Jerusalem described **in Revelation 21:10-27?**

> **You will be a crown of splendor in the Lord's hand, a royal diadem in the hand of your God.**
> **Isaiah 62:3**

14) How does God respond to the heavenly Jerusalem (**verses 3-5**)?

> **For the Lord has chosen Zion, He has desired it for His**

> dwelling, "This is my resting place for ever and ever;
> here I will sit enthroned, for I have desired it."
> Psalm 132:13-14

15) What is the proclamation in **verse 11-12**? See also **Isaiah 40:10** and **Revelation 22:12**. What do you think is His reward?

16) What will God's people be called in **verse 12**?

> But you are a chosen people, a royal priesthood, a holy nation, a people belonging to God, that you may declare the praises of Him who called you out of darkness into His wonderful light.
> I Peter 2:9

You have heard the expression that a house is just a house. A house becomes a home with the love shared by the people who live there. The heavenly Jerusalem, with all of its splendor, is nothing without the people who will dwell there. **Now the dwelling of God is with men, and He will live with them. They will be His people, and God Himself will be with them and be their God (Revelation 21:3).** God is not passionate about a city. He is passionate about us, His people. The beautiful city is His gift to us! Re-read **verses 3-5** and let God speak His words of love directly to you.

> The Lord their God will save them on that
> day as the flock of His people.
> They will sparkle in His land like jewels in a crown.
> How attractive and beautiful they will be.
> Zechariah 9:16-17

17) **You will be called sought after** or **sought out (verse 12).**

Because of His overwhelming love for you, God is relentlessly pursuing you. What did Jesus tell us about the Kingdom of Heaven in **Matthew 18:12-14**? How do you respond to such love?

> You who call on the Lord give yourselves no rest,
> and give Him no rest till He establishes Jerusalem
> and makes her the praise of the earth.
> Isaiah 62:6-7

> For Christ died for sins once for all, the
> righteous for the unrighteous,
> to bring you to God.
> I Peter 3:18

> Praise be to the God and Father of our Lord Jesus Christ!
> In His great mercy, He has given us new birth into a
> living hope through the resurrection of Jesus Christ from
> the dead and into an inheritance that can never perish,
> spoil or fade—kept in heaven for you, who through faith
> are shielded by God's power until the coming of the
> salvation that is ready to be revealed in the last time.
> I Peter 1:2-5

> Many, O Lord my God, are the wonders You have
> done. The things planned for us no one can recount
> to You; were I to speak and tell of them,
> they would be too many to declare.
> Psalm 40:5

> Send forth Your light and Your truth, let them guide me, let
> them bring me to Your Holy Mountain, to the place where You
> dwell. Then I will go to the alter of God, to God, my joy and
> my delight. I will praise You with the harp, O God, my God.
> Psalm 43:3-4

Before you go: Consider how the Lord specifically revealed Himself to you today. What words or phrases caught your attention? How do you respond to this? Lift a prayer of praise to the Lord.

Further Thoughts:

Please read **Revelation 21:10-27 – 22:6**. What do you look forward to in our heavenly home?

The Final Fulfillment

Lesson 19: Isaiah Chapters 63-66

This week's memory verse:

> **Our Father in heaven, hallowed be Your name. Your kingdom come, Your will be done on earth as it is in heaven.**
> **Matthew 6:9-10**

Before you begin: Please start by praying to God. Give Him praise. Ask Him to reveal Himself and to speak to you today through this lesson.

Please read Isaiah Chapter 63.

When Jesus Christ the Savior returns, He will gather His people to Him and then He will defeat the enemy forever.

> **See, your Savior comes! See, His reward is with Him, and His recompense accompanies Him.**
> **Isaiah 62:11**

1) Compare **verses 1-6** with **Revelation 19:11-21**.

> **At that time, they will see the Son of Man coming in a cloud with power and great glory.**
> **Luke 21:27**

> **In the hand of the Lord is a cup full of foaming wine mixed with spices; He pours it out, and all the wicked of the earth drink it down to its very dregs.**

Psalm 75:8

2) God has abundant mercy. His compassions toward us are unfailing. Describe the emotions and actions of God in **verses 7-9**.

3) What is God's name in verse 16? What do these verses tell us about our relationship with God? **John 1:12-13** and **Romans 8:14-17**.

> "I will be a Father to you, and you will
> be my sons and daughters"
> says the Lord Almighty.
> 2 Corinthians 6:18

4) What do we learn about our Heavenly Father from the following verses?

Matthew 6:14—

Matthew 7:7-11—

Luke 15:20-24—

Hebrews 12:5-11—

> How great is the love the Father has lavished
> on us, that we should be called
> children of God.
> I John 3:1

Please read Isaiah Chapter 64

God describes Himself as our Heavenly Father. As a father, He loves us, provides for us, disciplines us, and He forgives us.

5) How is God's power described in **verses 1-3**? What is the response to God's actions? How does **Joel 2:1, 10-11** describe this event?

6) To whom does God help according to **verses 4-5**? What did the Psalmist learn in **Psalm 40:1** and **Psalm 77:11-12**?

> **So, Christ was sacrificed once to take away the sins of many people; and He will appear a second time, not to bear sin, but to bring salvation to those who are waiting for Him.**
> **Hebrews 9:28**

7) How are our sins described in **verses 6-7**?

> "Come now, let us reason together," says the Lord. "Though your sins are like scarlet, they shall be as white as snow; though they are red as crimson, they shall be like wool."
> **Isaiah 1:18**

8) **Verse 8** states that God is our Father. What is the other image given depicting our relationship with Him? What do these

verses tell us about this relationship?

Genesis 2:7—

Jeremiah 18:6—

Ephesians 2:10—

9) What did our Heavenly Father do for us according to **Romans 5:8-11**? And what should be our response according **to I John 1:9 – 2:2**?

> **You will call and I will answer You; You will long for the creature Your hands have made. Surely then You will count my steps but not keep track of my sin. My offenses will be sealed up in a bag; You will cover over my sin.**
> **Job 14:15-17**

Please read Isaiah Chapter 65.

There are two groups of people described in this chapter, those who seek God and those who do not, those who will be blessed and those who will suffer God's wrath.

10) What angers and distresses God in **verses 2-7** and **11-15**? And what will be the consequences of their behavior?

God desires us to seek Him. He calls out to us. Can you feel His longing? **For I called but you did not answer, I spoke but you did not listen (verse 12).**

11) What does God promise to those who seek Him (**verses 8-10**,

13-15)? What do we learn from the parables Jesus taught in **Matthew 13:44-46?**

> Blessed are they who keep His statutes and
> seek Him with all their heart.
> Psalm 119:2

> But seek first His Kingdom and His
> righteousness, and all these things
> will be given to you as well.
> Matthew 6:33

12) How is God described in **verse 16**? What do we learn about this characteristic of God from these verses?

John 1:14, 17—

John 4:23-24—

John 14:16-17—

John 16:13—

John 17:17—

> Guide me in Your truth and teach me,
> for You are God my Savior,
> and my hope is in You all day long.
> Psalm 25:5

13) What does God promise in **verses 16-19?**

> Once you were alienated from God and were enemies

> in your minds because of your evil behavior. But
> now he has reconciled you by Christ's physical body
> through death to present you holy in His sight,
> without blemish and free from accusation.
> **Colossians 1:21-22**

> For I will forgive their wickedness and will
> remember their sins no more.
> **Hebrews 8:12**

> He will wipe every tear from their eyes. There will
> be no more death or mourning or crying or pain,
> for the old order of things has passed away.
> **Revelation 21:4**

Imagine, all of our past troubles, embarrassments and sins will be forgotten! Weeping and crying and pain and death will be behind us!

14) How does God describe our future home in **verses 17-25**? What aspects of the new heaven and new earth do you look forward to?

> For My Father's will is that everyone who looks
> to the Son and believes in Him shall have eternal
> life, and I will raise him up at the last day.
> **John 6:40**

> Very truly I tell you, the one who believes has eternal life.
> **John 6:47**

> And this is the testimony: God has given us eternal life,
> and this life is in the Son. He who has the Son has life; he
> who does not have the Son of God does not have life.
> **I John 5:11-12**

> Surely, You have granted him eternal blessings

> **and made him glad with the joy of Your presence.**
> **Psalm 21:6**

Please read Isaiah Chapter 66.

We have come to the conclusion of the Book of Isaiah. God tells us what is most important to Him in these final words, including another glimpse of our eternal home.

15) What does God tell us about Himself in **verse 1**? Where does He reside? What did Jesus say about this in **Matthew 5:34-35**?

> **He said, "Son of man, this is the place of My throne and the place for the soles of My feet. This is where I will live among the Israelites forever."**
> **Ezekiel 43:7**

16) What does God promise to those who follow Him (**verses 10-14**)?

> **And I—in righteousness I will see Your face; when I awake, I will be satisfied with seeing Your likeness.**
> **Psalm 17:15**

17) What does God promise to those who do not follow Him (**verses 15-17, 24**)? What does **2 Thessalonians 1:6-10** say regarding this?

> **The oppressor will come to an end, and destruction will cease; the aggressor will vanish from the land.**
> **Isaiah 16:4**

> But may the sinners vanish from the earth,
> and the wicked be no more.
> Psalm 104:35

18) What will happen in **verses 18-23**? What will be an offering to God (**verse 20**)? And what will we do (**verse 23**)? What does Jesus teach in **Matthew 25:31-46**?

> Blessed are those who wash their robes that
> they might have the right to the tree of life and
> may go through the gates into the city.
> Revelation 22:14

19) As we contemplate all of this, are you ready? Is your heart right before God? Are you anxiously waiting for what God has prepared for us?

> May the God of Peace, who through the blood of the eternal covenant brought back from the dead our Lord Jesus, that great Shepherd of the sheep, equip you with everything good for doing His will, and may He work in us what is pleasing to Him, through Jesus Christ, to whom be glory for ever and ever. Amen.
> Hebrews 13:20-21

> The hour has come for you to wake up from your slumber,
> because our salvation is nearer now than
> when we first believed.
> The night is nearly over; the day is almost here...
> Romans 13:11-12

> At that time, they will see the Son of Man coming
> in a cloud with power and great glory. When these

> things begin to take place, stand up and lift up your
> heads, because your redemption is drawing near.
> Luke 2:27-28

> The Spirit and the bride say "Come!" And let
> him who hears say "Come!" Whoever is thirsty,
> let him come; and whoever wishes,
> let him take the free gift of the water of life.
> Revelation 22:17

There is one more thing. Did you notice it? It is the message all throughout the Book of Isaiah. **For when I called, no one answered, when I spoke, no one listened (verse 4).** God calls to us and speaks to us. He longs for us. He wants us to listen to Him, to seek Him, to run to Him, to thirst for Him, to trust Him, and to worship Him. He prepared a way for us to spend eternity with Him. He is our Emmanuel, God with us. We are the beloved maiden who searched for her Lover and when she found Him, she clung to Him and would not let Him go. That is God's deepest desire.

> And I heard a loud voice from the throne saying,
> "Now the dwelling of God is with
> men, and He will live with them.
> They will be His people, and God
> Himself will be with them
> and be their God."
> Revelation 21:3

Further Thoughts:

1) Read **Psalms 45-48** and note the references to the end of time when God reigns in His Holy Kingdom.

2) What were the favorite ways God revealed Himself to you in these lessons? Why?

3) Read **Philippians 1:9-11**. This is the prayer I prayed for you investing in this study. How has this prayer been answered in your life during this study?

4) God with us. His ultimate desire is to be with us and us with Him. Consider the following words: close companion, special bond, rich friendship, intimate confidant. How has your relationship with God deepened through this study?

5) What changes, if any do you need to make in your life, with your relationship with God or with others?

**How awesome is the Lord Most High, the
Great King over all the earth!
Psalm 47:2**

APPENDIX

Communion Message for Lesson 16, Isaiah Chapters 53-55

> *"Man of God,*
> *Lead her like Abraham,*
> *Fight for her love like Jacob,*
> *Care for her like Boaz,*
> *Love her like Christ."*
> --Author Unknown

Lead her like Abraham. Hmm, yes Abraham was the patriarch of our faith. And when God told him to "Go!" Abraham went. But I question the leading of his wife Sarah. You may remember, Abraham passed Sarah off as his sister, not once, but twice, leaving her vulnerable and unprotected. But then again, Abraham and Sarah did find comfort in each other's arms when Abraham was 100 years old and Sarah was 90, and little Isaac was the result. Don't we all desire an enduring love?

Fight for her love like Jacob. Jacob was not perfect. But he adored and cherished Rachel. He worked hard labor for seven years for her and when he awakened the morning after his wedding, there was Leah, Rachel's older sister. What did Jacob do? He worked another seven years for his bride. Don't we all want someone to cherish us and to fight for us, and to be our hero? We want that knight in shining armor to ride in to save us. When the enemy throws a dagger at us, we want someone to come between us and protect us from that dagger.

Care for her like Boaz. Of all the men in the Bible, I could fall in love with Boaz. He was kind and generous, wise and wealthy. He did not just give orders to his workers; he worked right along with them. And when the foreigner, Ruth came to work in his fields, he took care of her and kept her safe. Boaz not only took care of Ruth and then married her as her Kinsman Redeemer, but he also took care of her mother-in-law Naomi. If you find a man who will take care of your mother, you are truly blessed. Don't we all want someone to care for us, in the way we want to be cared for?

Love her like Christ. Love her like Christ. Please turn with me to Ephesians chapter 5. This is a directive to men, but there are rich truths I want to show you. Ephesians 5, starting with verse 25. **Husbands, love your wives, just as Christ also loved the church and gave Himself for her.** Christ loved the church and gave Himself for her! Jesus Christ loves you and gave Himself for you. Verse 26, **That He might sanctify and cleanse her with the washing of water by the word, that He might present her to Himself a glorious church, not having spot or wrinkle or any such thing, but that she should be holy and without blemish.** Jesus' blood cleanses you so that you may be presented holy and radiant without blemish before Him. Verse 28, **So husbands ought to love their own wives as their own bodies; he who loves his wife loves himself. For no one ever hated his own flesh, but nourishes and cherishes it, just as the Lord does the church.** Jesus nourishes and cherishes you as His own body. Verse 30 **For we are members of His body,** (we are members of Jesus' body) **of His flesh and of His bones. "For this reason, a man shall leave his father and mother and be joined to his wife, and the two shall become one flesh." This is a great mystery, but I speak concerning Christ and the church.** Jesus desires us to be one with Him. One mind, one heart, one spirit, one purpose. Jesus prayed in John 17:20-21, **I do not pray for these alone, but also for those who will believe in Me through their word; that they all may be one, as You, Father, are in Me, and I in You; that they also may be one in Us.**

Let us read again from Isaiah chapter 53, starting in verse

4. **Surely, He has borne our sorrows; yet we esteemed Him not. He was stricken, smitten by God, and afflicted. But He was wounded for our transgressions. He was bruised for our iniquities. The chastisement for our peace was upon Him. And by His stripes we are healed. All we, like sheep have gone astray; we** have **turned, everyone, to his** own **way; and the Lord has laid on Him the iniquity of us all.**

We are all like an unclean thing, and all our righteousnesses are like filthy rags. (Isaiah 64:6) (like a menstrual cloth).

For our transgressions are multiplied before You, and our sins testify against us. (Isaiah 59:12).

For He made Him who knew no sin to be sin for us, that we might become the righteousness of God in Him. (2 Corinthians 5:21).

God demonstrates His own love toward us, in that while we were still sinners, Christ died for us. (Romans 5:8).

He who did not spare His own Son, but delivered Him up for us all. (Romans 8:32).

Oh, the deep, deep love of Jesus! His love is enduring, more than Abraham. He fights for our love, more than Jacob. He cherishes us and cares for us, more than Boaz. **He, Himself bore our sins in His own body on the tree, that we having died to sins, might live for righteousness—by whose stripes you were healed.** (I Peter 2:24).

Satan threw a dagger at our soul and Jesus came between us and took the dagger Himself.

In Isaiah chapter 54, our Lord takes this deep love further. He entered into a sacred, covenant relationship with us through the blood of Jesus and proclaimed ownership of us. **For your Maker is your husband, the Lord of hosts is His name.** (Isaiah 54:5). **I swore an oath to you and entered into a covenant with you, and you became Mine, says the Lord God.** (Ezekiel 16:8). We are His bride, and He is our Bridegroom. He expects our exclusive devotion and allegiance to Him and He becomes jealous when we turn our hearts away. As our Husband, the Lord loves us unconditionally with deep compassion. He provides for us, protects us, forgives us, and promises to come back for us to take us to His home so that we can be with Him forever.

In Isaiah 55, our Lord calls us to Him, to enter into sweet communion with Him and we become one with Him. We remember His sacrificial, enduring love for us, and we recommit our lives to Him. The Oxford Dictionary defines Communion as "the sharing or exchanging of intimate thoughts and feelings. It is a sacramental, spiritual or symbolic act of receiving the presence of Christ."

And He took bread, gave thanks and broke it, and gave it to them, saying, "This is my body which is given for you: do this in remembrance of me." Likewise, He also took the cup after supper, saying, "This cup is the new covenant in My blood, which is shed for you." (Luke 22:19-20).

Whenever we take communion, we remember Jesus' sacrifice for us. We eat the bread that reminds us of His body given for us so that we might live.

Have you ever wanted to see or touch Jesus? This communion bread is just bread, so we are not to worship it, but it does represent Jesus for us until we enter heaven. With this bread, we can see and touch Jesus. **Taste and see that the Lord is good**. (Psalm 34:8). When you place the bread in your mouth, let it melt on your tongue. **The two shall become one flesh**. (Ephesians 5:31). One mind, one heart, one spirit, one purpose. Jesus said, **For the Bread of God is He who comes down from heaven and gives life to the world . . . I am the bread of life. Whoever comes to me will never go hungry and whoever believes in me will never be thirsty . . . I am the living bread that came down from heaven. Whoever eats of this bread will live forever. This bread is My flesh, which I will give for the life** of the world. (John 6:33, 35 and 51). **Listen to me and eat what is good, and your soul will delight in the richest of fare.** (Isaiah 55:3). **My soul will be satisfied as with the richest of foods.** (Psalm 63:5).

We drink the juice as a reminder of the blood Jesus shed for us for the forgiveness of our sins. We have been washed in the blood of Jesus and are now presented as pure and holy before God. Jesus said, **"Let anyone who is thirsty, let him come to Me and drink."** (John 7:37). **Whoever eats My flesh and drinks My blood remains in Me, and I in him.** (John 6:56). **Oh God, You are my God, earnestly I seek You; I thirsts for You, my whole being longs for You in a dry and parched land where there is no water.** (Psalm 63:1). **As the deer pants for streams of water, so pants my soul for You, O God. My soul thirsts for God, for the Living God.** (Psalm 42:1-2).

When we commune with the Lord, we share intimate thoughts and feelings with Him. We renew our commitment to the Lover of our Soul, our Bridegroom, our Husband, our Savior, Jesus Christ, Emmanuel, God With Us. We receive the presence of Christ.
Let us pray.

Precious Lord Jesus, Lover of our Soul, we are in awe of Your love for us. How can we even comprehend such love? As we share this Communion with You, we remember Your sacrifice for us. We remember the amazing, enduring love You have for us. We, your brides recommit our lives to You. Please help us to love You with all of our heart, with all of our soul, with all of our mind and with all of our strength. Please help us to remain faithful to You and the sacred covenant between us. We betroth ourselves to You for all our lives. In Jesus' precious name we pray. Amen.

NOTES:

Lesson 7. Cynthia Heald; "I Have Loved You: Getting To Know The Father's Heart." NavPress 01/15/2013. URL: 9781617479168

Lesson 18. Randy Alcorn; "Heaven." Ytndale Momentum 10/1/2004. ISBN 0842379428.

Appendix: New Oxford American Dictionary; Oxford University Press 08/2010. ISBN 9780195392883.

Scripture quotations taken from The Holy Bible, New International Version, NIV.

Copyright 1973, 1978, 1984, 2011 by Biblica, Inc.
Used by permission. All rights reserved worldwide.

www.ingramcontent.com/pod-product-compliance
Lightning Source LLC
LaVergne TN
LVHW022322080426
835508LV00041B/1928